Writers as Teachers / Teachers as Writers

Also by Jonathan Baumbach

THE LANDSCAPE OF NIGHTMARE:
Studies in the Contemporary American Novel

A MAN TO CONJURE WITH: *A Novel*

WHAT COMES NEXT: *A Novel*

MODERNS AND CONTEMPORARIES:
Nine Masters of the Story (edited with Arthur Edelstein)

Edited and with an Introduction by **Jonathan Baumbach**

Writers
as
Teachers

Teachers
as
Writers

Holt, Rinehart and Winston   *New York*   *Chicago*   *San Francisco*

Library of Congress Catalog Card Number: 70–117284

First Edition

Designer: Winston Potter

SBN: 03–085048–7 (Hardbound)
SBN: 03–085049–5 (Paper)
Printed in the United States of America

"Teaching Writing" by George P. Elliott, reprinted
by permission of College English and George P. Elliott.
"Look Ma, I'm Teaching," by Ivan Gold, reprinted by
permission of E. P. Dutton & Co., Inc. From Sick Friends,
copyright © 1969 by Ivan Gold.

v

Contents

*Anyone who has passed through the educational
system of America is to an unconscious degree
near half a parrot.*
—Norman Mailer in *Armies of the Night*

1

Introduction

JONATHAN BAUMBACH

I

Students, in bid for student power, want voting say on curriculum at Brooklyn College—an issue of contention presently at most universities. There's nothing there, I tell them, not much, not enough. It's not the curriculum that matters but the teacher. They nod, offer arguments to convince me otherwise. I nod—it is an indication that I have listened. We fail to convince each other. One can't tell one's children anything (or one's students), can't save them from deception or death, though one quixotically tries. That quixotic gesture is what teaching—particularly the teaching of writing—is about.

The question comes up: "Can writing be taught?" The questioner of course knows the answer in advance, the question implying the answer—"No, it can't." Ah then, what are we all doing in the classroom? The best we can, I should hope, since nothing—nothing worth knowing (nothing beyond the banality of facts)—can be taught. It is what every serious teacher finally discovers. And it is after that discovery that the most valuable experience in the classroom can take place. This book, considerably different from my original conception of it, is about how ten diverse writers who teach make sense to themselves of their roles as teachers of writing —ten incomplete answers to the question. As Paul Goodman points out in an article in *The New York Review of Books* (April 10, 1969), "To be educated well or badly, to learn by a long process how to cope with the physical environment and the culture of one's society, is part of the human condition." He goes on to say that for the most part learning takes place incidentally rather than programmatically. "Generally speaking, this incidental process suits the nature of learning better than direct teaching."

Teaching in college, if one is serious about it, can be a frustrating, often heart-rending business. Success in grade school and high school in America is dependent on a tour de force of deceptions, the most serious of which—sometimes fatal—being denial of self. Middle-class education indoctrinates to perpetuate the system, prepares the student to be a responsible member of middle-class society with its emphasis on rhetorical high-mindedness based on preconceived reality—the totemistic notion that what one doesn't talk about (squalor, corruption, institutionalized inhumanity, complicated sexual feelings) doesn't exist. To succeed in our schools one has to learn to lie with a straight face and the easiest (most satisfying) way of living with it is to believe your own lies. Thus: corruption. School reality tends to be shadowless, made up of rights and wrongs, in literature no less than mathematics, though so boring and illogical that one needs the teacher's intercession to get to the truth.

"I have a right answer in my head," teacher says in the shared code language of gesture when he asks a question. The successful strategy is not to think through the problem but to psych-out what teacher has in mind—the right answer. The "good" student is quick to learn that different teachers, particularly in subjective studies, have different right answers in mind. I recall a time, teaching Freshman English at Stanford University—this, some ten years ago—when the director of the course had two student essays mimeographed and asked us, his staff, to grade them. The range in grades was extraordinary, shocking—considerably wider, I suspect, than even the director had anticipated. For the same paper—so it sits in memory—a student would have gotten an F from one instructor and a B from several others. And doing away with grades, offered from time to time as a general panacea, would not in this case have made much difference. The F man would have made it clear in his comments that he thought the paper failing work, while the B man would have indicated that he thought there was more good about the paper than not. Beyond the extremes, there was little consensus on either paper. Though we all had standards, we generally valued different things. The paper that generated the major controversy was about Hawaii where the author had spent some time as a child, was extremely fluent, had almost no technical errors, and read like a travel brochure. The B man could argue that the essay, though somewhat trite in idea, was excellent mechanically, lucid, and well put together. The F man, on the other hand, was outraged at the emptiness of the piece and argued that the fluency of the writer only made the essay more deplorable. "He'll never learn to write," says F (I'm inventing his dialogue here), "if we let him get away with glib bullshit." It is not diversity of standards which worries me but the extraordinary self-dividing pressure on the student when he has to accommodate himself from one class to the next to opposing authoritarian notions of good work. There are teachers (though I hope no longer) who fail students for making the same spelling error on two consecutive papers and others who are unconcerned with mechanical errors if a paper in their view has substance.

I don't think a piece of writing ought to be graded if only because the grade's importance becomes inflated, adumbrating the writing experience itself. The student writes to get a good grade (whatever that means in a particular context) and is not concerned with saying what he has to say, with speaking in his own voice. When students discover that I don't grade papers, inevitably some are upset because they don't know, as it seems to them, where they stand. For too many students, the grade (a symbolic accommodation to a reality) is the reality itself, the only goal that matters. It is the message of the system from top to bottom, disguised in euphemistic rhetoric, but there for any shrewd boy or girl to discover.

Success in school on all levels—for the moment, let's set aside the exceptions—is in a complicated variety of ways dependent on giving teacher what he wants. *What do you want?* obliging students in colleges are forever asking, frustrated by the apparent changes in the rules of the game. Students who have been successful in school through various strategies of deception, are often incapable when they get to college of finding their own voice, of even knowing where to look. Fortunately for the success mills (unfortunately for the life of the soul), few college teachers, despite lip service to the contrary, want the real thing, want the truth, are willing to allow the student his own perceptions when in opposition to their own way of seeing. Giving teacher what he wants is only a more ingenious and sophisticated game in most college classrooms and after a short period of acclimation the "good" student tunes himself into what is wanted. Education from top to bottom in America, with still rare exception, proliferates mediocrity. Severely limited teachers, filled with the best intentions of a self-limiting education, stunt students in their own image—none of whom, teachers and students alike, operating at even twenty-five percent of their potential intelligence. Added to the problem of a rigid, life-evading school system—an education for bureaucrats and technocrats—is a world which has been changing at astonishing speed, and we see an educational system which is, at best, irrelevant (that student word for our time), at worst, in opposition to almost every reality around us and so productive of a national schizophrenia. The dread fact is, American schools educate for genocide. Universities are in crisis (are under siege) because they are the freest and therefore the most vulnerable of our institutions; they are in symbolic hostage for the rest—elementary and high schools, city halls, police stations, court rooms, the military, the Pentagon, the government. . . .

II

I have deliberately overstated the problem, though not I think by much. Kids are resourceful, less fragile than one thinks, and find ways of surviving the system more or less intact. To come back to the issue of this book—what it is to teach writing in college—some of the most interesting (or potentially interesting) students are secret outlaws, shooting the deer of the king in private Sherwood Forest. A college writing class is a place to talk to the real person, the secret outlaw hiding out in the "good" student. One can't reach the outlaw (the artist) by merely asking him to come out of hiding or by offering amnesty. He's been around cops and teachers too long for that. There are obvious things to be said. If a student is distrustful, wary of revealing himself, one has to prove oneself trustworthy—whatever that entails—to bring him out. It could take years. One doesn't have that luxury—one has five months, sometimes ten.

The first job of a beginning writing class—creative or expository —is to get the student in touch with himself, to help him find his voice (see John Hawkes's account of the Voice Project experiment). One way is to give assignments that deny him his old strategies of evasion, that force him to work with a particular memory or sense experience. Almost all good teachers, I imagine, do something of the kind, though perhaps not. The styles of good teaching, one discovers, are as unique and various as the styles of good writing. The question follows: what is a good teacher? Most of us who teach have some idea and pattern our practice in configuration of the idea, seeking to fulfill the definition by example. One thing is certain—good teaching can't be programmed—a personal, human matter (not many left us)—which is why there are ten essays (by writer-teachers of widely varied practice) in this book and not one essay. Since you can't really *teach* a student anything—you can impart information, which is something else—what one wants (what I want) is to create an occasion where students can come to discovery, a classroom situation which creates occasion for discovery. I wish I could define exactly how it's done but by definition occasions for discovery are undefinable. What it comes down to— and on this point all of the contributors to the book seem to agree— a writing class needs to be a community. In the same way that a serious novelist, for example, must learn how to write a novel each time out as if he's never written one before, a teacher ideally ought to be a new teacher in each class he teaches. Of course, one learns from prior successes and failures—probably more from failures— but such knowledge is in the blood. One's successes can't be imitated successfully.

Students are frightened of failure, of making fools of themselves by being wrong, so develop self-defeating success strategies. The culture has little patience with failure, though if one doesn't risk mistakes, one severely limits the possibilities of growth. I've seen intelligent students in literature classes shut themselves off, become literally stupid rather than live with an experience that's not wholly comprehensible to them in other terms. There's always a review book or a teacher around to say what it's all about, to give the right answer to what is apparently a senseless puzzle. Why make a fool of oneself for nothing, for no practical gain? The system, one learns soon enough, rewards energetic caution. It may sound, talking about the teaching of literature here, as though I've strayed from my subject. I suspect that the teaching of writing and the teaching of literature are two aspects of the same concern. What we think of in the heavy breath of respect as literature, teachers and students ought to remind themselves from time to time, was once "creative writing" and was made by someone of the same species as ourselves. This goes (or ought to go) without saying but is often overlooked in the treasure hunt of academic analysis. It isn't that great books of the past are irrelevant to our time, as some students are claiming today, but that they are too often taught with the best of intentions as if they were alien jewels—moon dust.

Writers know, or ought to if they haven't been brainwashed by reading ingenious discussions of their own work, that they don't write novels or poems or stories with secret meanings. Yet students arrive in my literature classes with an arsenal of critical trowels, ax handles, magnifying glasses, manure separators, in grudging ar- cheological quest of "the secret meaning." I am all but certain that no sophisticated teacher of literature talks about "secret meanings" as such, but then where does this notion come from? High schools? Is it in the air? They must be getting the message from somewhere. No wonder when school is out and they can read what they want, our students almost never read for pleasure the authors they "learn" to read in courses. The books they read on their own, the honest ones admit, are for the most part subliterate popular novels (best sellers)—Harold Robbins, Irving Wallace, Leon Uris—which unlike the works assigned for the good of their souls in class are "easy to understand." No wonder serious writers want to teach—apart from financial needs and the pleasures of teaching. We feel—at least I speak for myself—that our schools are educating the young to be unable to read our books—that is, serious, difficult works that are considerably more accessible than classroom situations let on.

To begin with, it is not necessary to understand everything about a piece of writing to live with it. The author doesn't understand it all himself. The writing process is not the same for all of us but is, more or less (depending on who you're talking to), intuitive, which is to say that it is pointless to try to make sense in other language of the mysteries of a work of art. Teachers—I think we are all guilty of this at one time or another—tend to justify their presence by making works of literature seem incomprehensible without their intercession. And so a game evolves. Students accommodate their instructors—it is what is expected—by pretending helplessness in the face of slightly complicated texts, by pretending to be unable to read. After a point the pretense becomes a reality.

In my own view the teacher's role in a literature course is to make himself unnecessary. The question is how. One way is to stop talking about poems, stories, and novels as if they were inhuman artifacts to be analyzed and decoded. We ought to make it clear that the books we give students to read were written to be read for pleasure—the author sharing his vision of things—and not (specifically) to be talked about in English classes. Students must learn to trust their own responses. Once a student doesn't have to worry about not understanding—that is, not being able to translate the experience of a piece of writing into other terms—he can begin to get some pleasure from the books he previously hated. He has to be able to admit he hates them before he can begin to like them. Some students have been brainwashed to say they admire everything they know is supposed to be good—the strategy of telling the

teacher what he wants to hear—so they never permit themselves to
get in touch with a book at all. The guns that keep them in line,
that frighten them on occasion into what seems like near idiocy, are
grades (the possibility of failure) and being wrong, not seeming to
understand what is obvious to everyone else. It took me a long time
as teacher to admit there were things in novels and poems that I
didn't understand or couldn't translate coherently into other language. My admitting my own limitations made it possible for my
students to admit theirs, took some of the awful burden of having to
be right off their backs. The deepest, most valuable experiences are
insuperably difficult, often impossible, to put into words. Which is
what art is about, is it not? Making sense of the mysteries of our
lives.

I find writing easier to teach than literature mainly because
writing classes tend to be smaller and therefore more susceptible of
becoming a community. The two experiences—reading and writing,
teaching reading and teaching writing—are intimately related. One
learns to read in new ways in a writing class if only by coming in
touch with process, by discovering for oneself that the making of
literature is a human act. The greatest service of a writing course is
not the developing of professional writers—no course can do that—
but giving a student a visceral sense of what literature is.

Almost every writing course I've taught—no matter what the
level—the first papers turned in were mostly dreadful. They were
mostly dreadful in more or less the same way—cliché-ridden, full of
lofty sentiment, melodramatic, cautious, frightened, empty. Many
of these students, who seemed near-hopeless at the start, turned out
after several months to be gifted writers. (Some, I was to learn,
had written well before.) Other teachers I've talked to have had
similar experiences. Something in students' educational experience
—what it is, I suspect, is at the heart of the problem—makes it
hard for them to write well (to be themselves) for a new teacher.
Two obvious reasons: fear of risk (What does he want? Too early
to know); awareness, not always conscious, that the system values
improvement. It used to be standard procedure in freshman English
programs for the instructor to give low grades on early "themes"

regardless of quality so that the student would have impetus to improve. This has been discredited as psychological prod and is less prevalent—"truth" presently held in high esteem—as overt or implicit practice. I suspect, nevertheless, that it has been in the air so long at every level that students tend unconsciously to regress each term to make possible the improvement teachers like to see. How do we know we've taught them anything unless we see improvement? The successful student plays to the vanity of his teacher, both collaborating to perpetuate the myth that something called education takes place in schools.

What started out as a collection of casual notes to myself has turned, I'm afraid, into a heavy sermon. The point is, as any student revolutionary will tell you (as if one needed to ask), institutional change in our society moves exceeding slow. Despite present questioning of even the most sacred givens of educational theory, it's not likely that we'll see much change in the next few years in public education on elementary and high school levels. Which puts as one can see, as one *is* seeing on campuses all over America, an enormous burden on the college to somehow right past wrongs. The best we can do, which is where a writing class begins, is to help students unlearn bad habits. A writing teacher has to fight against years and years of systematic depersonalization to get to what's unique and alive in each of his students—the real voice as opposed to what John Hawkes calls the "voiceless" written language of our schools.

Colleges like to make distinctions between creative writing and what they call expository writing (also called Freshman English). There are, I've discovered—after years of believing the myths—no sensible differences as disciplines between them. Good writing is the communication of one's vision of an event, the sharing of it, between writer and reader. Most freshman writing courses are, in effect, vocational courses in academic disguise. If after twelve years

of schooling an eighteen-year-old hasn't learned to write a gram-
matically correct, coherent, formal essay—good old institutional
voiceless prose—he obviously doesn't want to learn how, has for his
own good reasons determinedly resisted learning how. Give him a
course in writing business letters and be done with the pretense. In
the expository writing program I taught in at Stanford (1958–1960)
—I'm sure the course has changed considerably in recent years—
students wrote themes of "Definition," of "Comparison and Contrast," of "Classification and Analysis," using Logic (1) deductive,
(2) inductive, ending up with two informal essays (1) "The Writer
Looks at the World," (2) "The Writer Looks at Himself." And we
English teachers claim that sociology is a non-discipline. Not to
belabor the point any further, what is said in this book about the
teaching of creative writing holds true for the teaching of expository writing. These essays are about the indirect and direct
relationships between the process of writing and the teaching of
writing (as process). Intention is one of the central issues. Students,
like the rest of us, will make themselves understood when they want
to be understood. Obfuscation clearly has its own uses. Witness: the
prose of politicians and advertising men, of media in general.

At Brooklyn College I teach a course called Introduction to Creative Writing and a more advanced course called Short Story
Writing. When I started teaching I used to write myself an outline
(like lecture notes) of what I wanted to cover during the hour.
Now I prefer not knowing, trusting to instinct, improvising, listening, discovering. It's something like removing the net from a high-
wire act. Essentially, I teach pretty much the way I go about writing
a novel, leaving things open within limited bounds of control for
as long as I can stand it. If it does no other good, it keeps me
interested in the proceedings. At the same time, I don't pretend to
abdicate the prerogatives of authority. I know more about writing
than students do, though of course they know things that I don't
know, and to pretend otherwise (a currently fashionable modesty)
would be a form of deception. If one wants students to be open to
experience as writers, as teachers one has to, to some degree (no
easily resolved issue, this), set them an example by being open

oneself. In the past, students have justly accused me of being less open with them than I expect them to be with me. I am as open as is comfortable with me, as is natural.

One thing I've been doing the first days of class for the past four or five years, no matter what the course, is have students answer a series of questions about their interests. I've never learned very much about them from their answers—only occasionally is a student willing to be honest on such short acquaintance—but I continue to ask. My sense is that I ask the questions not to find out where they're at, as I used to think, but to have the questions in the air. Though I improvise new questions each term, the essential question behind the questionnaire is—*what matters to you?* It is where they begin as writers, where at least they ought to begin.

I try various assignments—different ones each term—at the beginning of a course to prod students into writing about things close to them. The more restrictive and specific the assignment, the better the papers generally, though not always. Many students resist writing from experience, insist that they have to make up stories because nothing of interest has happened to them in their lives. Even so—who am I to tell them otherwise?—they must do the assignment.

I have them read good stories that deal intimately with ordinary experience, stories about sex, death, family life, growing up—if only to show them that subject matter doesn't have to be exotic for a story to be fresh. Often, the problem is that the very things that matter most to a young writer are things he's afraid to expose to paper, very normal feelings and experiences which he nevertheless conceives (as a product of respectable middle-class education) as perverse and shameful.

Let's talk about a specific class—generalization is too easy. I collect twenty short narratives about a childhood humiliation. Most of them turn out to be commentaries on an experience and not evocations of it. The experience has been forgotten, repressed, denied, and what comes out is the "cover story"—the publicly acceptable version—a false memory. I read the best ones to the class and poll responses, withholding my own (though sometimes giving it away despite myself) until everyone has his say. (As an issue of faith, I never read a story to the class that doesn't have something admirable about it.) It is always a problem at the beginning of any writing class to get students to be honest with each other, particularly when they don't like something. I point out that they're not doing the writer a kindness but patronizing him by being uncritical. Gut reactions are often more valuable to the writer, to the life of the community—than so-called constructive criticism. Sometimes the author of a story will want to say something, explain his intention if he feels his story has been misunderstood. More often, the author merely listens in. I read stories to the class rather than have their authors read them because it seems to me useful for a writer to hear his work as if written by someone else and so hear it without its intentionality built in. Young writers sometimes think they've made something clear that's not on the page at all.

Gradually, even at a subway school like Brooklyn College, the writing class becomes something of a community. Not quite a community—they hardly know each other outside of class—but approximately one. Sometimes the term is almost over by the time it happens. For various reasons, few of which I can account for, about half a dozen students (before the term is out) write pieces remarkably better than anything they'd done before. The context of the class has something to do with what happens. Students are programmed to write *for* teachers, which is corrupting, I think, no matter how sensitive or intelligent the teacher. My students write for each other and finally, I hope, for themselves. The good stories read in class—and I tend to read only the best ones—excite other good work, make students aware of new possibilities of subject and treatment. One young writer's story touches a forgotten nerve of experience in another. At the same time, student discussions get increasingly rigorous and wise. The more vital the class becomes, the less I insist on my own role. In fact, when the class is working well, I (metaphorically) disappear, become the least active member of the community. Hemingway has said that what every good writer needs is "a built-in shock proof shit detector." The class serves as communal shit detector.

What takes place in the classes I've described are beginnings, openings up, and only rarely, finished (publishable) stories. I don't talk much about technique as such—perhaps if I knew more about it I would—disbelieving in formulas, assuming that every piece of writing has its own unique resolution. I don't tell students how I would end their stories if I had written them—unless they ask, and even then reluctantly. Sometimes I have beginning students do exercises in which they imitate the structure of a story they admire. It is useful in the same way a parody can be useful, though I have no special faith in any particular assignment. Some of the most successful writing classes I've had seemed to be going nowhere for the first five or six weeks. What matters is not any particular assignment or particular class but the cumulative experience of the course. (And there are generally three or four in a class—almost always girls—who seem to make no progress at all, too frightened or vulnerable to risk sight.) Universities are in crisis because (among other complex causes) of the depersonalization of the system and its inflexibility to change. The writing class is an oasis where students can make (create) sense of the disorder of their lives, share private experience with one another, without irrelevant pressure of grades and career and shame.

This book is a record of ten writers' experience as teachers. Few of us (probably none of us) became writers because of writing classes we took as students. Of course, there were fewer writers teaching writing in colleges when we were undergraduates, though I suspect that's a false issue. Becoming a writer (a hellishly lonely calling) has more to do with temperament and will than with gift or education. It may be that the very best a writer can get from a class is some small confidence, a sense of others in similar struggle. The very worst is to become dependent on someone else's judgment or authority—I've run into students (gifted ones alas) who are unable to produce unless you give them an assignment and a deadline. If anything, miseducation at the lower levels makes writing classes in college necessary. If a writing class is successful, it (ideally) makes further writing classes unnecessary. Finally, those

few who beome serious professional writers would likely have become writers without a writing course—perhaps it would have
taken them longer to discover themselves. A writing class (creative
and non-creative) is an academic rather than a vocational course—
an action course in the humanities—one of the rare school occasions
where the individual is valued for being uniquely himself.

2

Some Thoughts I Have in Mind
When I Teach

WENDELL BERRY

I

In the midst of so much easy talk about the "generation gap" I feel a certain unwillingness to admit that such a thing exists. Because I am not far past thirty and am in no special hurry to belong to the "older generation," I would like to assert that the generation gap does not exist for me in particular. And yet I am sure that in some manner it undeniably does exist and that it defines the predicament and the burden and the responsibility and the excitement of being a teacher. If it is not a generation gap—the phrase is often used to imply a difference in *kind* of experience, which I believe in only somewhat—it is at least a difference in the amount of experience and in the sense of possibility.

When I face my students I am increasingly aware of this difference. Between me and the seniors in my classes there is now a difference of about twelve years. These years, which lie before them in the largeness of possibility and ambition and hope, lie behind me, fixed and unchangeable, having come to some success, more failure, and no doubt mostly to trivia and waste which I have already forgot and will not think of again. My life has passed farther into facts than theirs.

In the last few years my life has become to some extent predictable. The future has become no less enticing and fearful than before, but now I know with some confidence what my concerns are and what they very likely will be for a long time. Both as a writer and as a man I have come to be surrounded by interests and meanings and tasks, and even a landscape, that I can think of as my own because the work I have done has brought me to them. My students' lives are not yet predictable in this way. Held off by the circumstance of school, in which they have had to make no permanent commitments, the future is still in effect whole before them. I have become what I am at the expense of the possibility that I might have become something else or something better. And for me, looking at my students, there is the sense of the imminence of this tragedy: they will realize a few of their possibilities at the expense of most of them. There is the inescapable awareness that there is more talent, more adventurousness, more spirit inside the university, than will be able to survive outside through marriages and jobs and parenthood and misjudgment and failure of nerve and bad luck.

And so, as I see it, the confrontation between teacher and student is essentially a confrontation between experience and possibility. It is exciting and often deeply moving to work and think and speak in the atmosphere of possibility that surrounds students. But in this there is also an irreducible bewilderment, for though one presumably has some measure of control over facts, and even over one's own possibilities, I think that one must be extremely hesitant and uneasy in dealing with possibilities that belong to other people. I would rather enlarge a student's sense of possibility than "direct" it. But this is personal, at least in its effect on the student, and insofar as it is personal it is problematic; there are no systems for it. Experience speaking to possibility has also the obligation to pass on some sense of what may be expected, a sense of the practicable, and at the same time to avoid condescension and discouragement. This is what I think of as the moral predicament of a teacher, and as it can have only particular solutions in the lives of particular students it remains a predicament, always as liable to failure as to success.

When this confrontation occurs in a classroom in a large university there are other difficulties. Such classrooms have come to be surrounded, and threatened with suffocation, by the administrative machinery. In my own university the administration, by the use of a great deal of expensive machinery for the sake of efficiency, has become omnipresent, inescapable, and monstrously inefficient, evidently limited in all its everyday functions by the mental capacity and the judgment of the IBM machines. I know of one simple problem, calling for the use of only the least bit of common sense, which our registrar's office has been consistently failing at every semester for three years, and which promises to be unsolvable. The major business of university administrations appears to be the production of useless work and waste paper, no item of which may be safely overlooked or detoured, and all of which is harassing and obstructive to teaching. The administrator thinks in terms of power and money and construction and reputation and prestige; what happens in the classroom, so long as it does not obstruct the running of the waste paper machines, is simply of no interest to him. The student feels all this more, and is more at the mercy of it, than the teacher. He can hardly escape the suspicion that as far as the administrators are concerned the result of his schooling is a series of holes in a card. If he does something that cannot be programmed it will either go entirely unnoticed or get him into trouble with the authorities. And the IBM machines can no doubt prove that all this is conducive to excellence and high character.

In addition there is the constant pressure to succeed: the student must take advantage of his college years to make himself known to the "right" people; he must leave the school with the qualifications for a "good" job. All the time the student is supposedly being educated the predominant influence on him is his prospective "place in society"—a pigeonhole, sucking at him like a vacuum cleaner. Far from receiving an enlarged sense of possibility, his own and humanity's, which I take to be what an education is meant to give, the student is narrowed and pinched by his preoccupation with success —with grades and with beating the system. But beating the system, to him, is likely to mean learning to cooperate with it so well as to be invisible in it. He is not being educated, but only *programmed* so that he will work without friction in his "place."

And so I have come to look upon the university as a machine that one must to a considerable extent work against in order to work within. The machine seeks an outcome that is altogether predictable: the student is to "learn" certain designated facts and procedures; the syllabus and the tests may all be written in advance.

But the teacher of writing is not concerned to transform the student into a finished product. He is concerned with possibility. He seeks to create an atmosphere and an expectancy that will encourage the production of work that he can neither foresee nor imagine—and that perhaps even the student can neither foresee nor imagine at the time he begins the work. What is only possible and cannot be foreseen obviously cannot be programmed. This intent to encourage and foster the unexpected, then, immediately sets the teacher of writing at odds with the machine. He finds that he must be constantly braced against the institutional slant if he is to teach at all.

My own experience suggests to me that this can be done with some success. Which, of course, depends on what one means by success, and I admit that I don't insist on overwhelming percentages. I attempt to apply the highest standards and to expect only a very few to measure up. My primary interest is not in raising the average, but in fostering excellence. If the exceptional are brought to excellence, then the average will have models.

At least in the circumstances I have described, I think that the best relationships of teacher and student are those that turn into friendships. In friendship the education machine is entirely circumvented and removed from consideration, and the two minds can meet fully and freely. The student comes to know the teacher, which in my opinion is a thousand times better than knowing what the teacher knows. The teacher ceases to function merely as a preceptor and becomes an example—an example of something, good or bad, that his life has proved to be possible.

The next best relationships, I suspect, are those that turn into hostility, for an enemy may do one the valuable service of exemplifying what one does not want to be. I now understand that my own education was much advanced by the examples of certain teachers whom I strongly disliked. And so I would not withhold myself from the possibility of my students' enmity any more than I would from the possibility of their friendship. Enmity defeats the machine as effectively as friendship and makes for vital contact. A student examines a teacher he dislikes with a sort of fascination, alert for faults and errors that will justify his low opinion. This can be a strenuous and exacting mental exercise, useful to both parties.

The worst students are those the education machine proposes as ideal: those who want only to be told what you want them to do, and then slavishly *do* it. These reduce teaching to a dutiful servitude, deadening and exhausting to the teacher because they do not respond; they absorb everything and give nothing back. The minds of several of these can form an abyss into which a teacher's very life can disappear for whole hours.

II

My aim as a teacher, as I have said, is to angle at large in the realm of the possible, to be always responsive to *what might be*. There is little chance of system in this, if by system you mean an ordered progression laid out in advance. If it goes as I think it should, there is no knowing what will happen next. It is when my students begin to go beyond what I expect, surprising and informing me, that I think the work is succeeding.

I base nearly everything I attempt on one assumption: that every person's experience is in some way different from anybody else's. Hence, everybody has something to tell me that I would be interested to know. The student's task is to find out what it is and to write it well.

I also assume that the work done in a writing course can be of use to a person who does not become a "writer"—which, of course, applies to most students. There was a time when I thought a writing course was a *special* kind of exercise, and therefore I had some doubts that it could be justified as a part of a college curriculum. I have changed my mind. My doubts were based on the propaganda which assures us that we have achieved widespread literacy in this country. I think that substantial evidence could be produced— from business letters, from the written work of college seniors, from published books and articles by experts of various sorts—to show that we have not yet done so by any means. "Education" has licensed the old forms of illiteracy and invented several new ones.

Though I have no system, there are nevertheless certain things that I always attempt to do:

1. I encourage the students to read. It is surprising how many believe that they can write before they have read, which is like thinking you can talk before you have heard speech. The written language comes from the spoken and remains under its influence, but it also comes from and remains under the influence of other writings. Since we now live nearly all the time in the atmosphere or in the reach of prepared language—*written* language—we must choose either to be influenced intentionally by the best or inadvertently by the worst. If one does not know the *Iliad* or *War and Peace* or *Doctor Zhivago*, then one is susceptible to the influence of those movies and TV serials which insinuate that war is productive exclusively of comedy and sexual adventure. If one does not know Faulkner or *Huckleberry Finn*, then one is susceptible to the influence of *The Beverly Hillbillies*. If one does not know the poets, then one is susceptible to the influence of advertising jingles and government propaganda. I believe that we need more than ever to look on literacy, the knowledge of books, not as a polite accomplishment or social ornament, but as a moral necessity, a form of moral self-defense.

2. I try to read aloud in the class everything that is written by the students, making exceptions only when asked to do so by the writer, or when a student writes so far beneath his ability that criticism would be of no use to him. I think this reading aloud gives the valuable experience of listening critically to language and causes the students to reckon with the results of the exposure of their work. I invite the class to comment, asking those who speak to be as precise and specific in their judgments as possible and to

answer any arguments that may be raised against them. I usually reserve my own comments until last and hope that somebody will disagree with them. Like a lot of teachers, I am made uncomfortable by the authority that many of my students insist on conceding to me. I dislike the feeling, in the classroom or anywhere else, that somebody is supposing that I speak with absolute authority, that I *have* to be right, that my word *has* to be the last. If I don't feel free to be wrong, and sure that someone will try to correct me if I am wrong, then to say anything at all begins to seem too great a risk. As a teacher my major complaint is that I am too seldom challenged.

If a student's work is so bad or absurd as to be funny, I find it is relieving to go ahead and laugh. This gets rid of the constraint of politeness, which is meaningless in this situation anyway, and feeling free to laugh appears to free the laughter from unkindness.

3. I constantly attempt to encourage perceptiveness and accuracy —the use of the intelligence, the imagination, the senses. To me the aim of literacy is to have a language capable of telling the truth and of responding freshly to experience. Clichés are literally blinding: if a person is willing to *say* the current clichés about progress, for instance, the chances are great that he will *see* nothing else. Instead of an experience he will have a pseudo-experience—the agreed-on abstraction represented by the cliché—which means that both the person and the society are denied the use of his intelligence. He will not know whether he is telling the truth or not, for having accepted the judgments implied in the cliché he is no longer in reach of the evidence. I am anxious to have the student thoroughly examine a thing or an experience both before he describes it and *while* he describes it. I am anxious to have him realize that the act of describing in words is a part of vision that will help to clarify what he sees, and even lead to the discovery of aspects and details and relationships that he would likely not have seen otherwise. A pencil in the hand can give a power and focus and reach to all the faculties that they do not have without it. That is, the act of writing, at best, is not simply the execution of something already

prepared in the head, but an act of discovery. For these reasons I usually ask beginning students to write two short assignments a week, one for each meeting of the class. This is to free them from preconceptions about "creative writing" and to get them to looking at things. It also gives a space limitation, which ought to suggest some of the possibilities inherent in editing, rewriting, and self-criticism. An instruction of this sort assumes that the students are all industrious, interested, and cooperative, and so one should be prepared for failure in varying amounts. After some weeks of these short assignments I tell the people to write in any way they want to. At this point usually some quit entirely, some do worse, and some do better.

4. I have spoken above of accuracy in the observation of detail, which I think is indispensable both to good writing and good think-ing. But there is a perceptiveness which depends on that, and fol-lows from it, and is more valuable: that is the sense of form, the form both of the thing being written about and of the thing being written. The sense of form has to do with the discovery of relation-ships within experience and with the discovery of the way con-sciousness moves into and among these relationships. Language is both the instrument of the discovery of form and form's graph and embodiment. Form cannot be predicted, but only made, and so it is impossible to tell how to make it. In teaching, one is limited to showing examples and to pointing out failures. In a given piece of work it is possible to say whether or not there is a coherent form and whether or not the form is of any interest or value. It is possible to say what is arbitrary or irrelevant. But it is impossible to say what *ought to be* the form of work that is formless.

5. The teacher should do everything possible to encourage, and even enforce, careful use of the materials of writing: the words and the sentences. This may be the basic obligation of the writing teacher, and for me it is often the most difficult. I think I am usually too lenient about it. But illiteracy among the "educated" is the worst form of slobbishness and should not be tolerated any-where. In a writing class it is an outrage, and it suggests a pre-

sumptuousness or a foolishness on the part of the student that is outrageous. The teacher has a right to expect that a student who enters a writing class will have some competence in diction and spelling and punctuation and grammar and syntax. The student who lacks this competence should be considered, not wrong or deficient, but simply absent.

III

But I must return again to a question that I have asked myself over and over, and always have to answer in a way that bewilders and troubles me: can one *teach* writing?

I don't think so. And I suspect, moreover, that most things worth knowing cannot be taught. I am depressed and repelled by the thought of all the books and articles that have been written to tell people how to write—all that stuff about how to get "the reader" interested in writing that (presumably) does not deserve his interest, as if the art of writing were merely counterfeiting. What gets my interest is the sense that a writer is speaking honestly and fully of what he knows well, and it is stupid to think that he could have received this power from a book or a teacher. It is a power that he has made in his life by the practice of his art and attentiveness to his experience. No good book was ever written according to a recipe. Every good book is to a considerable extent a unique discovery. And so one can say with plenty of justification that nobody knows "how to write." Certainly nobody knows how other people ought to. For myself, though I think I know how to write the books I have already written—and though I guess, wrongly no doubt, that I could now write them better than I did—I am discomforted by the knowledge that I don't know how to write the books that I have not yet written. But that discomfort has an excitement about it, and it is the necessary antecedent of one of the best kinds of happiness.

As a teacher there are certain things you can *do*. Encourage accurate observation. Encourage reading. Insist on competence and care in the use of the language. Criticize and invite criticism. But though these things can be exemplified and learned, I doubt that they can be taught. And even supposing that they can be taught, none of them leads directly or with any certainty to any result that can be predicted.

And these, furthermore, represent only the narrowest and smallest function of the teacher. His great function, or opportunity or obligation, is to manage somehow to address himself openly and generously and invitingly to the unknown—the *possible* that presents itself to him in the minds and lives of his students.

To me the hope of becoming, as a teacher, more than a mere mechanic of facts and procedures lies in the awareness of the lives that produce the work and that are, in turn, to be served by the work. I believe that the most meaningful calling, for both teacher and student, is not the making of a product—not even a great book —that will be worthy of the attention and interest of other people, but the making of a life that will be worthy of *one's own* attention and interest. The highest creativity, as always, is to come to a sense of the amplitude of life and the largeness of possibility. In our own time the most necessary and useful act of creation will not be to produce a great work of art, but to imagine and implement a meaningful alternative to the pigeonhole—the narrowly specialized and all too well prepared "place in society"—that the education machine offers as a goal, but which is really a dead end and a death.

I think there is a good chance that the best result of a writer's teaching may be wholly inadvertent. His greatest service to his students may not be anything he *intends* to do for them, but in his chance revelations of himself. As his readers, they may learn more or less of what he has written. As his students, they learn more or less about *him*. In one way and another he exhibits his responses, his tastes and judgments, his interests, his ways of thinking. He brings a mind somewhat formed and prepared by what he has experienced and written into the presence of minds less formed and prepared. It may be that in his teaching role his mind serves best as a sort of artifact. The students come upon it as archeologists come upon a prehistoric skull buried in its native place, among its effects. They sit and ponder it and make various responses to it. They may mistake its nature or its meaning. They may misunderstand it entirely. But if they are intelligent and conscious and responsible, they may be enlivened and enlarged by their pondering.

3

Writing

ROBERT CREELEY

Some years ago I was trying to buy a truck in Boston, and the salesman after some conversation asked me if I might be available to tutor him, to "improve his English," as he put it, so that he might secure a better job. I think that habit of attitude toward the fact of speaking, and writing and reading equally, is deeply ingrained in anyone who passes through our usual system of education. There is a sense adamantly present that a "right" way and "wrong" way exist and what one is trying to teach and/or learn is the *correct* approach. But writing, insofar as I've had to do with it, is absolutely hostile to such an assumption. There can be examples obviously, facts of writing one responds to and respects, and these become the literal measure of one's own practice. Such measures are, however, inevitably personal, no matter how much they may seem instances of general or topical interest. Millions of people may be involved by what Bob Dylan is saying, but the more significant point, for me, is that each one hears him as a singular occasion.

That, in fact, is one of the delights of writing, that it involves such a one-to-one relationship. At least its most active possibility lies for me in that fact. I know that many people may reach college with a marked resistance to writing, but again, assuming that they have been subject to the *right* and *wrong* emphasis, it seems very evident that writing as a discipline has been used primarily against them. Even when they've done it *correctly,* the effect is most often a complete generalization of their own concerns, and what hopefully they began with—some explicit fact and their own relation to it—has become "correct usage" only.

Of course language, *a* language, is a system, and acquaintance with the nature of that condition is most useful. But what a difference there is between the usual college grammar text and such a book as Ernest Fenollosa's *The Chinese Written Character as a Medium for Poetry*—or Gertrude Stein's notes on parts of speech in "Poetry and Grammar"—or Edward Sapir's *Language*. Clearly these represent my interests, and I cannot assume their relevance for another—but the point is, I would like to, and in teaching I would absolutely depend on texts having explicit involvement with language as a system rather than the generalized "rule books" all too frequent.

But this gets the cart before the horse, just that in teaching writing, or any other possibility, one begins with the students themselves. If I speak French and they speak Chinese, no communication occurs. It's not indulgence that argues the use of knowing the terms and active content of those one proposes to teach. So, then, "why write?"—and is any possibility to be found in it that they themselves value? What do they read, if they read? What uses do they find in writing, if any? Is it an activity merely demanded by their various courses—reports, analyses, explanations, etc.

Don't be discouraged if, at first, nothing much happens at all. I was once in a writing class taught by Delmore Schwartz, who began with the reasonable assumption that there must be *one* writer that all of us respected in common. Unhappily there wasn't—and the class sat in that dilemma for the full length of the semester. It isn't that he was wrong or right, but rather that *any* assumption about what can or should happen must yield to the actual situation. Most frequently the people one is trying to teach will have been habituated to feel that reading and writing are activities having as necessary purpose the gaining of a didactic information, and in a class which, hopefully, is not intended to center upon a "subject," or to make known specific content of such order, a significant number may well be disgruntled, feeling that the course is a waste of time. Others, proposing more sympathetic interest, will want immediately to know what ways of writing will be most useful to their intentions and will expect to be taught these in a rather literal manner—with appropriate notes as to adequate and inadequate "performance." I'd suggest that both attitudes be balked—there is nowhere one is necessarily going, there is really nothing more to say than what seems of interest to them at the moment, and if no one has such interest, then that's true—for themselves as well as for you.

If such a way of beginning appears to be extraordinarily lax—granted that writing is, in one sense, a discipline of very complex and actual particularity, do remember that one's own interests and commitments in no way involve the possibility of others until those others have entered their condition. My excitement will only be an irritation for anyone who finds himself neither sharing my situation of experience nor my own commitment to the terms of the activity involved. How, then, engender such circumstance as makes a common ground?

First of all, begin with what's there—by which I mean, the literal fact of the people. You can ask them "what they want to do" and may well get the answer, "nothing"—but that's enough, i.e., push that, "what is that state of activity," or literally *do* nothing, if that is chosen as the state of possibility. In such a situation the one thing most dulling seems to me to insist that such and such is a "great" book or that this or that way of writing is most "effective" and to argue consequently, but only with oneself, all the possible justifications.

You may choose to impose upon them the necessity of writing something—there is obviously no reason not to—but don't limit it too didactically to a "subject" and don't look for what you think it *should* say. The dreary habit of parroting so prevalent in contemporary education comes of such insistence, and profits no one at all. Take what *is* said as the context and use that as the means of exchange. You cannot apply to an alternative or to a rule you may respect, which the writer himself has not experienced. In other words, make known to him that what he is saying has the possibility of this or that extension—*not* that what is unknown to him is a constant and frustrating limit.

Having once taught the first grade, I can remember that lovely experience of witnessing someone's coming into the possibility of reading and writing, so that the literal fact of speech gains extension in time and space in immeasurable senses. It is an absolutely *human* delight, and if people have forgotten that, it may well be due to the fact that this incredible agency has been so hedged in by impositions of *purpose*, and necessary *meaning*, and all manner of didactic insistence. As if the only point in learning how to swim were to get from A to B . . . Poets were once called "makers" and the word *poetry* comes from a root meaning "to make." But *what* to make—despite all insistences to the contrary—is as viable as language and human condition can make manifest. It's hardly permissive to want to return some of that possibility to senses of teaching and learning.

In fact, that seems finally the point—that unless writing does become that pleasure, it remains a drudgery and only an occasion prompting more criticism, more "doing it wrong." How to make it such pleasure no man can easily tell another, nor can one assume that all people will share equally in its delights. But you don't have to kill it. You don't have to humiliate and ignore and find contemptible what may be the very possibility you are committed to foster. I am sick to death of "taste" which wants to convert all experience to terms of fashion and the social. Rather, respect Pound's "Damn your taste! I want if possible to sharpen your perceptions, after which your taste can take care of itself." Your own are involved as well as those of your students.

How you do what you do remains your own possibility, and invention. It may or may not involve books, newspapers, films, television—or any fact of activity possible to your life and that of your students. Writing is an activity, not a subject. You cannot propose an isolated area of its relevance.

What follows, then, is an instance of my own involvement with teaching and writing, specifically with poetry—although writing is, for me, all that is made with words and written down.

11. *Contents of Poetry**

What Allen suggested, and what I thought would be a good idea, would be to begin with some sense of writing in the most literal of possible contexts. Now the supposition, I suppose, on the part of some of you who've come, is that we write poetry; in other words, this is what we do. And we, in effect, have been given a definition publicly as poets. We've published books and all the rest. But that kind of qualification is something I'd not like to take on, in this or any other context. So I would like to take up the issue of writing as a physical act. What I will tell you is how I write, and Allen, then you take it from there, you do the same. In other words, I want to speak of what is involved in writing for me.

When I first met William Carlos Williams, for instance, I remember he took me upstairs to show me where the bathroom was, and as we went by the—I think the bedroom—he showed me the desk that had been in his office when he was in active practice; and he showed me his typewriter, which was a large old office machine, and the way it fitted under the desk; and he showed me the prescription pads that he used to use. And again, Allen and I were thinking of how the qualification of the size of the paper, for example, will often have an effect on what you're writing, or whether or not you're using a pencil or a pen. Habits of this kind are almost always considered immaterial or secondary. And yet, for my own reality, there is obviously a great connection between what I physically do as a writer in this sense, and what comes then out of it. So I want briefly to qualify it. I was curious to know how I do it

---

* This text has been transcribed by George F. Butterick from a tape made by Fred Wah at the Vancouver Poetry Conference, Wednesday morning, July 24, 1963, and was first published by *Audit* (1968). The speaker of the italicized portions is Allen Ginsberg. I am the other speaker.

myself, in the sense of what really do I do. Well, say, first of all, I write always with a typewriter. I get very nervous about using a pen, because pens run out of ink in a way . . . ball points are what I would use, as and when I do write that way . . . pencils have to be sharpened, I get so involved with the sharpening of the pencil. Also, I think it goes back to a sense I had when younger, that type-writers, typewriting, implied a "professional" context. If you were going to be serious, or going to *claim* seriousness for yourself, the instrument that you used in writing had to be particular to what the act of writing was. So that I had, I think, a basically naive sense of this kind. I wanted to be able to do it with a typewriter. Now, equally, I never learned to type. So I mean my typing is a habit that's developed, with two fingers. I never took a class in high school or any other place that taught me how to use the full, you know, all your fingers when you're typing. Think again, that begins to be a qualification of how *fast* I can write. In other words, I find that the pace of my writing is concerned with the speed with which I can type. Now, I can type actually about as fast as I can talk, with two fingers. I find, for example, if I have to work on somebody else's typewriter, I'm displaced, because there may be a slight varia-tion in the space between keys. I find that now I can use the type-writer I do use without looking at it, so that I can be thinking of something without consciously wondering where my fingers are. I find . . . let's see, I want to keep on a little bit in this sense of what the physical conditions are . . . because again, I started writing in a context where I was embarrassed. I didn't want to bother any-body. I didn't want, you know, like, don't mind me, but just go right ahead with what you're doing, with your *serious business*, with your serious preoccupation. This was primarily in a former mar-riage, and the problems thereof . . . I didn't want to call attention to myself, because doing that might force me to define what I was trying to do—which is obviously impossible. So, the next thing I would do would be to create a context in which there was a residuum of noise, constantly present, so that my own noise wouldn't be intrusive. And so I find often I turn on the radio. I used to—back in New Hampshire, where I think I really sat down

to think of how to write or what to write—I used to play records
all the time. We had at that time, I remember, one of these big
Jensen speakers and all, and amplifier, and I'd put on the records
that I then much valued, as Charlie Parker and what not—but just
because that rhythmic insistence, I think, kept pushing me, I kept
hearing it. And lately for example, in the last year, I finished a long
prose work, a novel, and I found that what I was writing could be
actually stimulated by playing particular kinds of music. In other
words, I don't know . . . I'm not a psychologist or even interested
in this aspect, what I'm . . .

What kind of music?

Well, for example, the
whole first part is written primarily to an old Bud Powell tape, a
record, where you get these great kinds of almost concert style . . .
let's say a poor man's concept of beauty, you know, where you get
these great crescendoes of sound, and where you get actually a
basically simple melody, as "I Got Rhythm" or anything, playing
through this, and then you get this involvement that constantly
comes back to the simple statement because it's embarrassed actually with its own hope. So this first part of the novel is written
in that sense. Then the whole middle section is written primarily to
John Coltrane, where you get deliberate dissonance and you get
fragmentation—I wasn't conscious of this—and then the last part is
written to a kind of Nancy Wilson, you know, where you get a
"where love is gone," dig? And you get a *real slick* pretension. In
other words, where she's singing, in effect, the memory of some
authenticity which she no longer even . . . she never meant it. I
saw her on television and . . . she's no slicker than any professional,
but she's singing in a manner which is now a *manner*. She's not an
innovator, as was Sarah Vaughan, or, more particularly, Billie
Holiday. Again, the middle section involves Billie Holiday. But
what I'm trying to say is: so, that's a physical requirement for me. I
find it very useful for me . . .

Even in poems?

Even in doing any-
thing. It gives me something to focus on or to relax back into as a

place where I feel safe. Anyhow: the typewriter, the insistence of music, rhythm, something with a strong rhythmic character, not *too* loud, subtle enough so that you can always go back to it . . . and paper. Usually an 8 x 11 sheet. I best like, most like, the yellow copy paper that's not spongy, but has a softness to it, so that when you type, the letter goes in, embeds a little. I hate a hard paper. When you erase this paper you take a layer off. And I remember again—now this is why I want to point out, this is not ridiculous— because I remember one time when living in Spain, there was none of this particular size copy paper that I was used to using. So I got a legal size sheet. And it was a suddenly a terror, because I would finish what was normally my habit of dealing with the paper and realize that I had about six inches left at the bottom that was blank. This set up a whole different feeling. I remember writing a story actually using this paper, and it seemed to me that things were taking an awfully long time. In other words, the whole balance or pattern of the way of working with the thing was being changed. So the paper is significant. Again, Allen and I were talking about the way Jack Kerouac . . . the qualification of his writing that occurs when he is working in small notebooks. Or could I say the same of Robert Duncan, for example, who uses a notebook and writes in ink, and the composition of his books is obviously done as he's writing. There is, for example, an actual instance of a book of this kind that he did, called *Fragments of a Disordered Devotion,* in which it's reproduced from the actual . . . well, actually he wrote it as a copy of his own manner. It's an imitation of his manner by himself, so it has that. . . . But you realize that it's all happening visually as well as intellectually or mentally. Olson, in his letters . . . you begin to realize Olson's spacing, the ordering of where things occur in his thought. He'll begin a letter like, "dear so and so," and then start with the information, and before he's, say, halfway through the page you've got these things jumping all around . . . the movement, is moving, trying to locate like, let's put that there . . . no don't, now this goes there, oh but you can't forget that . . . but you can't forget this too . . . you can't put them like that, be- cause it's a lie, they don't exist that way, you've got to . . . He's trying in effect to give the *orders* of thought—in no pretentious sense—and a typewriter for him, for example, is something that has much defined his habits of writing, as he said himself in *Projective Verse*. But equally, he has a speed in handwriting that's fast, a very fast style of writing. . . .

But positions and textures of papers, envelopes and what not . . . I find again that in order to be taken seriously by myself that I again had to create a context in which I could exhibit the instance of professionalism. I remember some friend, for example, who said he always washed his hands before he started to write, because he wanted to be clean, he didn't want to get anything dirty. I can remember equally, when I had run out of paper . . . the circumstances of living at some remote place . . . I would really get . . . it would be awful. And then you'd start to improvise paper from envelopes —but very carefully folding them and all but ironing them out to get the right feeling. What I'm trying to say with all this rambling, is that the particular habits of writing that you begin to develop will have, curiously, a great significance for what you write. If you think I'm fooling, you might for example try to see what happens if you write with different kinds of media. In other words, try writing with large crayons, or—I wish we had access to this—it would be interesting to see what happens if you try to write on something the size of this blackboard. I taught first grade also . . . I remember this . . . where you're writing things like [moves to blackboard] . . . I could do this, in teaching handwriting. . . . Now, I can't write like this, I get so absorbed, involved with the voluptuousness, the sensuous . . . it's distracting to me. Because what I'm trying to do, if I'm successful . . . I am not anticipating what I'm thinking, I am not anticipating any content before it occurs. At the same time, I'm trying to recognize, or rather, I'm awfully bewildered by confusions between certain terms—the states of consciousness—e.g., the difference between recognition, understanding, realization, knowing. I'm trying to describe a state in which one primarily feels what is happening as a fit balance. If you do things like ski or swim or drive, for example, you know that sense of feeling when the car is operating smoothly, when the balance of the steering and the movement of

the car is coinciding with an intention of your own and is following with a sense of grace, an appropriateness. Everything is, in
effect, falling into place. You're not intentionally putting it there,
but you're recognizing the feeling of its occurring there. So that
when I'm writing myself, if something becames dissonant or something becomes jarred, arbitrarily, then I have to stop. One other
thing I should note, also about the sense of the physical act of
writing, is that the same habit of wanting it to be "perfect" in its
appearance, means that if I'm writing and I make a mistake, I take
the paper out and copy it down to that point, correct the mistake,
and then throw the paper away. In other words, I have a great
difficulty writing on the paper. For example, I can never write in
books. And I get awfully upset if other people write in my book . . .
writing in my book . . . seeing dirty hands all over my book . . .
Because I don't really think that I can own a book. I don't think
that I have the *right,* to write.

In college itself . . . now let's go back there, because that's
where we are again . . . I was in the context of other younger men
of that time who wanted to be writers also . . . Donald Hall, for
example—that was in Harvard in 1946, a group which then centered around *Wake*—Seymour Lawrence, now editor for Atlantic
Monthly Press, Kenneth Koch. I remember, say, Kenneth Koch one
time invited me up to his rooms for, I think it was sherry, and to
listen to records, like Bach and what not, and to read me a few
poems. Well, I can remember going up to his room, and it was, you
know, it was a very comfortable room. Kenneth comes from a
family that has money, and so that was evident in his room. It had
very tasteful reproductions, there was furniture that he'd bought . . .
I couldn't do that. At that time I wasn't writing anything that I felt
was that significant. I mean I was desperate to understand what
would actually be a poem. Again, as Allen and I and were talking yesterday—you've really come at a good time!—because I think each
of us in our own circumstances has come to that point where the
very definition of a poem as a possibility, not as a possibility perhaps, but as an actual construct, is something we are very unable
to state like that. In other words, I cannot define a poem. It's a

curious state of mind to have arrived at. I cannot tell you what I think a poem is. I think that has to do with the facts that all the terms of consciousness are, at the moment, undergoing tremendous terms of change. We were again talking, thinking of the context now in the States. There is an alteration of a very deep order going on in the whole thrust or push of the consciousness, literally the Negro consciousness, that has been for years relegated to a kind of underside or underworld. As Duncan says, "I see always the underside turning. . ." Well, see, the Negro personality in the States has been forced to live in this underside world, except in contexts which he could control. LeRoi Jones, for example, grew up in a fairly secure middle-class background that had, let's say, the securities of that status. But you see, there was always a limit to it. You could always take one step beyond the control of the neighborhood and you were suddenly in a world which was utterly unresponsive to your reality. Now this reality, which has become *the* dominant reality in the States today, is the Negro reality, it is not the white reality, it's the Negro reality. You may want to interpret the activities of the Kennedys as large, liberal recognitions that have been long overdue, but I think it would be utterly naive to do so. I think that the Kennedys are being washed along in a shift that is not only located in the States but—now Allen can tell you much more accurately these terms—but is coming from a whole shift of controls and communication terms that are actually centered in Africa and Asia.

I don't want to take us too far afield, but my point is that the very premise on which consciousness operates is undergoing modifications that none of us I think are at the moment capable of defining. We can only recognize them. Let's say, that if Pound says artists are the antennae of the race, I think that any of us here is in a position to be responsive to this feeling that's so immense, so definite, and so insistent. Not because we can *do* anything with it. It simply is, it's a big change, it's a deep change in consciousness, and I'm curious to see what's going to happen—which is a mild way of putting it. Indeed! But you have a poem, Allen, in which you say, "Where all Manhattan that I've seen must disappear." And this for me is what is happening in the States in a different relationship, in a different context—where all the terms of consciousness that I grew up with must disappear, are disappearing momently, daily. The terms of reality are changing. Even the terms of this course are changing . . . by which I mean, this course would have been impossible ten years ago, by definition. Senses of writing would have been impossible to present in this fashion ten years ago. We were, happily, involved with a reorganization of premise that gave us our particular occasion. Yours is going to be perhaps even more a mess. I mean that I think that the change which is occurring now is more significant than the Second World War by far, because it's the residue of that war in reference to the atom bomb and, equally, the shift in *all* terms of human relationship that have been habitualized since, oh God, thousands of years. This goes back to correct, not to correct, but to reorganize premises that have existed for thousands of years, concepts of person. . . . Look, I'd like you to talk for a while . . .

> . . . *the last time I wrote was on a train to Kyoto and Tokyo. I suddenly had a great seizure of realization, on a whole bunch of levels. I was thinking of a poetic problem which is not along lines. . . . It's another matter. Also, about an emotional problem which was just resolving itself. And I was suddenly having feelings for the first time, certain kinds of feelings for the first time in about a half year. I was feeling something that had been growing and growing and growing and all of a sudden appeared to me on the train. So I had to get it then because I knew in an hour when I got to Tokyo I'd be all hung up in Tokyo—you know, looking for a room in Tokyo—and I'd be having other feelings, or going back to material problems of arranging things. But here I had that moment and. . . . That's what I don't understand about your writing, what happens to you if you suddenly realize something—do you have to, arrange your paper? What do you do then, you lose it!*

You're right! No, I was just thinking as you were saying this, that the limit of my ability to write, at the moment, and has been for the last two years, is that I have to secure a physical context in which I can "work." It not only has to be qualified by having paper and the rest of the paraphernalia, but it has to have equally a social qualification. I remember, for example, friends walking in when I'm working. I literally stop. I cannot work when someone's looking at me. So that, I *envy* you. I remember . . . again this experience of knowing both you and Jack in San Francisco, and Jack equally will walk always with a notebook and be writing away. Or Robert Duncan, again. . . . That's why I suppose I always end up living in these circumstances that are very isolate, in other words, where I won't be disturbed. Yet I don't think it's a pretentious thing. It's frankly a need I . . .

       . . . *what you set up . . . does that actually catalyze feelings?*

    It seems to create a context in which those feelings can occur. The thing is that I'm so shy—in no specious or stupid sense—but I'm so worried about keeping myself together when I'm in public, so to speak, as even now. I mean these habits of speaking are, after all, the habits that I got from teaching. But when I'm writing, you see, that business of Olson's, "He left him naked, / the man said, and / nakedness / is what one means . . ." In order to be in that state of nakedness, I have to be where—it isn't so much distraction—but where I can open up this equally small thing, and feel it with the intensity of all the perception that I . . . that the ego bit can recognize, and then destroy the ego by its own insistence. It's shy in other words . . .

       Situated where there is no threat.

              Well, equally, it's an . . . see, I would be embarrassed for years. I remember when I got to the Southwest, the people there have a very easy and pleasant habit of embracing one another when they meet; that is, in-laws or friends. It took me *years!* I was, frankly, when I saw you for example, I was so pleased that I could put my arms around you as an old friend and hold on to you. It took me years to be able to do that, and maybe one day I'll be able to do this too. I'm not satisfied with the habits of limit that I've created for myself, because not only have I given myself a million excuses for doing nothing nine-tenths of the time, but I've created a context in which only—I realize now—only certain kinds of feeling can come. In other words, after all, when you've got the fort, like all the guns mounted and ready to blast until you're utterly safe, and you let out this little agonized thing . . . it skips around the room, you know, and you're embarrassed, you hear someone move in the kitchen, think O my God they're *coming* . . . no wonder the poems are short! I'm amazed that there are any at all! At the same time, you see, one is stuck with one's actuality, at the same time this is the only point I can begin, this is the place where my feelings are most present. I mean that in the sense of I have a horrible train-ing. . . . Olson speaks of being trained to speak, you know. He said that when he was a younger man—he's a very large man—and as a younger man he was . . . obviously must have been awkward, and his presence was a problem. He'd walk in, people would, like, duck, or they'd *respond* to him in ways that were not *particular* to his feelings at that moment. I equally had somewhat the same thing. I found that my feelings had an awfully bothersome quality for people I wanted to get to. God I'd, you know, I'd do anything to please them, and I found that I couldn't. I mean I couldn't in a way that I could depend upon. So that the poems anyhow began to be a way of dealing with things that I was otherwise prevented from having. Well anyhow a sense of security . . . I don't mean security in the sense of insurance or not being afraid. I think in those instances within that room all hell breaks out, as you well know, in the sense that everything is possible there in a way that. . . . Again and equally, if I walk on, if I'm sitting on the train with a notebook, I'm so self-conscious about it. Again this habit of my environment. I think what we're trying to do with all this is to insist to you that these aspects of what we're talking about are not immaterial. In other words these are the . . . I don't mean to give them undue significance or to . . . I don't want to qualify this way at all. What I'm trying to say is don't start thinking of writing as some particular activity leading to some particular effect for some particular purpose. It is just as relevant what size paper you use, as whether or not you think you're writing a sonnet. In fact, it's more relevant. And this aspect of your activity ought to be, you ought to be aware of it, simply that you should begin to feel as rangingly all that is issuing as a possibility and as a qualification of that possibility. In other words, if you want to write with a paper like this, please *do!* If you find yourself stuck with habits of articulation, try doing something else, try shifting the physical context. . . .

A Postscript

The preoccupations here evident were, in fact, more decisive than I could then have realized. I had trusted so much to *thinking,* apparently, and had gained for myself such an adamant sense of what a poem could be for me, that here I must have been signaling to myself both a warning and the hope of an alternative.

Not too long after I began to try deliberately to break out of the habits described. I wrote in different states of so-called consciousness, e.g., when high, and at those times would write in pen or pencil, contrary to habit, and I would also try to avoid any immediate decision as to whether or not the effects of such writing were "good." Some of the poems so written are to be found in *Words,* among them "A Piece," "The Box," "They (2)," and "The Farm." These were, however, still written on the customary 8 × 11 sheets and in the security of my usual home. But nonetheless they began to gain for me the possibility of *scribbling,* of writing for the immediacy of the pleasure and without having to pay attention to some final code of significance.

When *Words* was published, I was interested to see that one of the poems most irritating to reviewers was "A Piece"—and yet I knew that for me it was central to all possibilities of statement. One might think of "counting sheep"—and I am here reminded of Williams' poem, which Pound chooses to include in *Confucius to Cummings,* "The High Bridge Above the River Tagus at Toledo":

> In old age they walk in the old man's dreams
> and will still walk in his dreams, peacefully
> continuing in his verse forever.

To count, or give account, tell or tally, continuingly seems to me the occasion. But again I had found myself limited by the nature of the adding machine I had unwittingly forced upon myself.

Slowly, then, I came to write without the mechanic of the typewriter. I also began to use notebooks, first very small ones indeed, and then larger—and I found many senses of possibility in writing began consequently to open. For one, such notebooks accumulated the writing, and they made no decisions about it—it was all there, in whatever state it occurred, everything from addresses to moralistic self-advising, to such notes as I now find in the smallest and first of them:

> This size page forces the
> damn speciously gnomic
> sans need for same—
>   —it
>   it—

There was no hustle to argue the virtue of any possibility instantly, nor to do more than write, which same "freely" to do, as Remy de Gourmont in Pound's quotation of him insists, "is the sole pleasure of a writer." How long it took me to realize that in my own life.

It would be impossible to thank Allen Ginsberg enough for what he was somehow able to reassure me of—or to thank those other friends whose way of writing was of like order: Robert Duncan, Charles Olson, Denise Levertov, and the many others, who were wise, like they say, long before myself. It's lovely to do something with your bare hands and mind, in the instant it *is* possible, and finally I know it.

4

Teaching Writing

GEORGE P. ELLIOTT

I

Nowadays there is much discussion of a civil war that is said to be raging in American education. On one side are the powerful: the public school system, including nearly all administrators and teachers and reaching out through boards of education into the governing institutions of our society. On the other side are the weak: the children, a few teachers, possibly a very few administrators, and some champions such as Edgar Z. Friedenberg. The system (Bad) crippled the children (Good) to fit the requirements of this society (Bad) instead of setting them free to be creative (Good). Even according to this manichean Good/Bad scheme, things are a lot more complicated in college than they are in school. College students are not children any longer, though it is an American custom (Bad) to treat them as children. A lot of college teachers and even a few administrators are intellectuals (Good), so that in any halfway decent college the students, at least in the social sciences and humanities, are led to question (Very Good) the values by which America lives. Nevertheless, basically the same war is raging in the colleges as in the schools, because in both the ultimate power, money, is controlled by governing boards chosen from The Establishment, i.e., people important in business, church, and state.

In more activist moods, I pretty much accept this scheme. But now, wielding a pen—a tempering, cooling instrument of thought —I am made uneasy by it. Good/Bad makes me skittery. Children don't seem to me all that weak; they generate strong emotions both in themselves and in adults, and that is a considerable power. Their chief weakness, obviously, is ignorance; in addition to not knowing how the world is put together, they don't know how best to use their power—for which good reason the job of education is to give them some truths and no lies about how the world works and some training and advice about how to direct their powers to fruitful ends as well as to restrain them from sterile ones. I believe, like a proper liberal, that children are naturally creative and full of love and that everything possible should be done to let them grow up that way; but I also believe, after Augustine and Freud, that every child is a compendium of vices which must be controlled if he is to grow up to be a tolerable member of society. How to accomplish both these ends at once, I have no notion; I think they are ideals to be striven for, like justice and freedom, in the knowledge that they can never be attained and that to attain either would be to destroy the other. I believe that society, politics, the law, is a necessary evil ("Democracy," Churchill is supposed to have said, "is the worst form of government ever invented except for all those others"). That is, I do not see the loose federation of small true primitive communities dreamt of by idealistic anarchists as being a real option available to us; I see as far more probable the mere anarchy of nihilism, which I dread, or the totalitarian State of nihilism, which I dread quite as much. Finally, in this whole matter of school against child, society against the individual, I am suspicious of the metaphor of war. War, including civil war, seems to imply victory or at least a possible cessation of conflict, and it certainly implies an unhappy state of affairs disruptive of that most desirable condition peace. But I conceive struggle as being in the nature of human life, itself a source of vitality, never-ending; I do not see the combatants Law and Impulse as being in themselves just good or just bad, nor do I see the struggle between them (in any form, including School versus Child) as being just good or just bad. But I do see the alternatives to this struggle as being just bad. Such struggle could be eliminated on the one hand only by our annihilation, which is an unreality suddenly made actual in 1945, or on the other hand by our attaining utopia, which is equally unreal though genetics seems to be bringing it within the realm of possibility. In my view, utopia was a pleasant dream so long as it was clearly unobtainable because of our nature; but genetics may very well be giving us the power to change our nature, and that appalls me as much as does the power to exterminate ourselves which physics gave us. For even if we should endeavor to perfect ourselves by breeding out our destructive passions—and I see little reason to suppose that that would happen since we as we are now are the ones who must do the breeding—even so, I am against that endeavor, on the grounds that we are perfectible only in certain ways, not in all and that to make ourselves lopsidedly better is a form of denaturing, dehumanizing ourselves. I hope people don't decide to attenuate into Houyhnhnms, just as I hope they don't allow themselves to congeal into Yahoos: I hope they decide to remain human. And I don't take "human" as synonymous with "good"; Stalin was human, Martin Luther King was human, and so are you.

No one in his right mind supposes perfection is attainable in teaching college English, especially teaching writing. But it can be done better than it is commonly done now, and I have some ideas, derived largely from experience, about how to do it better. They won't effect an immediate and radical reformation of American institutions, for even figuring out how to start such a reformation is a full-time job and I'd rather teach and write; but they do involve subverting those institutions enough to get your work done, to teach better than you're supposed to.

My first teaching job was in a ratty private high school in Berkeley and, towards the end of my year there, I learned two things that have since influenced me a good deal. One was that it was the student's IQ more than his grades which decided our principal on whether to recommend him for college; indeed, she often changed grades, up and down, without consulting the teachers. Ever since discovering that, I have viewed grades, credits, admissions standards, degrees, nearly all that goes on in registrar's offices as mostly irrelevant number-jumble of the sort with which our lives generally are cluttered. The only trouble with this contempt of mine is that it was so easily come by and is shared so wearily by so many of my colleagues: the corrosions of cynicism. The other thing I learned happened in the midst of a class discussion of Blake's "Garden of Love." A diligent, worried-looking, phlegmatic C-student in whom I had thus far detected no spark of soul suddenly said, "I get it! Poetry's double-talk!" Light, and on a couple of other faces reflected light. I have no idea whether he has continued to read poetry or just how much I had to do with that moment but I know that such illuminations are among the high goods of teaching. I also know that the main contribution an educational system can make to such experiences is to get students, teacher, and books into a room together—not so much, though you can't do without it. Once you are in the room with some students, what practical measures can you take to produce such moments? I have never found out. Like instants of grace, they come according to a mysterious scheme over which we have only a negative control: we can keep them from happening by the relentless pedantry of legalism and factology, by denying imagination, by disciplined dullness.

The next year I got the deadliest teaching job I've ever had, teaching bonehead English at the University of California to freshmen who failed, as most did, an entrance exam in reading and writing. Syllabus, grammar, spelling drills, red ink, the works: it was a higher rigid system intending to remedy the deficiencies of a lower rigid system. It worked impeccably in suppressing imagination in all the Americans in my three sections, but I was lucky enough to have also a Mexican Indian who had begun to learn Spanish at the age of twelve and was only now, new to the States, beginning to learn English. He was as handsome a man as I have ever known, with the most intense gaze, and he turned in the livest writing I saw from a student for years, until I began to have near-professional writers in advanced writing courses. He wrote a prose-

rhapsody entitled "When Socialism Come to Mexico," which I
marked meticulously and graded 10 (10 was to F as F was to A).
In conference I talked to him about idioms, conjunctions, dangling
participles, the run-on sentence. He turned in another paper,
snatches of which I still remember, on the execution of Emperor
Mamilliano and G'ral Miramon. System to the teeth, I red-marked
it as before. I don't remember what else he wrote that term; nothing
much. I didn't feel particularly bad about this at the time: I was
busy with my own affairs; I had the merest glimmer of what
teaching could be. System makes many things easy, including hard-
ness of heart, and it safeguards the perplexed, the slothful, from
many dangers. It is here to stay.

After the war, I got a regular teaching job at St. Mary's College
near Berkeley. At the first faculty meeting of the year, the president
told us to "keep a united front against the students." The charitable
interpreted this, "don't knock your colleagues in front of students."
This seemed to me mere decency, and still seems so; it is not hard
to discourage students' impertinent probes; by your recommenda-
tions, you let them learn as much as good manners permit them to
know of your private opinions of other teachers. Maybe this is what
the president meant at that meeting, but it is not what he said. I
think he meant what he said literally, as too many others rigid with
system so mean it. However, I think no better of those who in effect
adopt the other extreme as a sort of motto for action, secretly keeping a united front with the students against the faculty. Teachers
and students should no more be like lovers, in my view, than like
guards and prisoners. They should be like parents and children:
authority *with* love.

Fortunately the president did nothing to unite us against the
students beyond telling us to, which united some of us, all right,
against him; in the classrooms we were free to use our authority
as we saw fit. (An indolent despotism leaves you far freer than a
diligent democracy: committees. At St. Mary's in those days, we
had no committees; next door in democratized Berkeley, the chan-
cellor appointed a committee to select the committee on committees.) Though I used that huge word "love" to suggest something

of the relation of teacher and students, I cannot claim to have
individually loved many of mine very much over the years, roughly
as many as I have hated. All the same, I began to notice, at St.
Mary's where I learned most of what I know about teaching, that
an odd thing kept happening in my classes—not in all of them, just
in those I felt to have been reasonably successful. At the beginning
of the semester, I would enter the classroom cold, stiff, full of system; I was ready to be disgusted by the ignorant indifference of the
students, their stupidity, their poor language. But sometimes, late
in the semester, I would look forward to going into the same classroom with pleasure, charged up by the students' energy, their improvement, their sprouts of imagination. I did not talk much about
this experience to other teachers, not wanting to seem boastful,
fearing it might be illusory or a symptom of some sentimentality
in myself. A Chaucer man helped me define it—the Chaucer men
I have known have tended to be wiser than most. You can tell a
good class, he said, by the way it pulls together late in the term
into a kind of community. He did not know how it came about or
what he contributed to bring it about; he did not think such a class
learned more in the testable way than another; but he felt, as I did
and do, that only such a class can be called successful. This is an
occasional community; a year later you can't remember most of the
students' names; there is no possible way of quantifying the experience, regulating it, reducing it to system. You do not feel
separated from the students by your authority in such a class but
united to them; you certainly do not personally love them all and
may even dislike some of them; yet not only is the experience of
such a fragile community a good in itself but also, as I believe, it
heightens the experience of literature, which is among other things
a form of communion. I have no practical measures to recommend
for achieving this happy condition. The ones I employ myself vary
from class to class, and none are foolproof. Recently here at Syracuse University where I have settled, I had two freshman honors
classes discussing the same texts, which I had chosen because I
was interested in those books at that time; ideal conditions, apparently; yet one class was a success and the other a total failure (to

complicate matters, the successful class contained the least cooperative student and the disastrous class the student who wrote the
best paper). But it is not just that I have no measures to prescribe;
I would not prescribe them even if I thought I had some. For it is
of the essence of community that its members make it themselves,
learn their own ways to make it. With each new class you must
strive for it all over again. Rather, since it is like love, is a kind of
love, it does not come by being striven for directly (the people I
have known who talked about "working hard at our marriage"
wound up divorced); the hard work goes into removing and pre-
venting obstructions, that it may come if it will and stay a while.

The most effective obstruction within a teacher's personal control
is knowing too well ahead of time what he is going to say. The first
lecture class of my career was surely the worst, not because my
opinions were disreputable or my knowledge inadequate but because I was so scared that I carefully outlined my lectures in advance; at the time I was speaking to the students, I was not thinking, much less feeling, what I was saying; I was repeating what I
had thought days or weeks before. You may be repeating the best
ideas of the best scholars and critics; you may be repeating opinions
you yourself generated spontaneously a year or two before; you may
be repeating lecture notes you jotted down thirty years ago. It matters, of course, how good the opinion is; but to utter opinions, even
the best ones going, without meaning them at the time you are
speaking is the surest mode of pedagogical contraception I know of.
System at its worst can do no more.

One day a few years ago a dear friend came to town, and we
stayed up till four in the morning talking and drinking. The next
day at ten past one in the afternoon, I walked into a classroom
with seventy or so students in it and began to talk about the Book
of Job. I knew it well, though I had not reread it for a long time
and had not taught it before. I had spent ten minutes looking
blankly at the text before class. I had only the foggiest notion about
what I was going to say, and seventy-five minutes to fill. What in
fact I did was to ask a central question to which I did not have an

answer in mind, explore all the answers I could think up and dismiss them one after another, and then with a minute to go come up with a good one. The stillness in the room that last minute and the opening of my voice as I said what came into my head constitute the finest classroom experience I have ever had. I discovered afterward that the answer I came up with was ancient and respectable, the sort of chestnut you'd expect to yawn over in a college-outline series; in fact, for all I know I had come across it long before and forgotten it. No matter: at the moment of talking I was discovering something worth discovering, and I was doing this because of the people I was talking to, for them and for myself at once. The closest thing to it in my experience is writing a story, as I have done a few times, the whole thrust of which is toward a final revelation which I know only when I get there. In Karl Shapiro's figure: "I paint myself into a corner and escape on pulleys of the unknown." That class of Job remains for me the model. Since then, I have constantly aspired to open the classroom door each time with my mind full of the text for the day, whether it is *Lear* or a student's first draft of a story, but empty of ideas about it, and then dive in. This method doesn't always work, of course, even for experienced teachers, much less for novices who are not yet saturated with their subject, but when it does, there's nothing better. I would rather fail at trying to teach this way than to have spent a lifetime successfully not-failing.

Spontaneity is all very well, you may object, for professors who only have to teach two or three courses a semester, courses pretty much of their own choosing, and who have sabbaticals to refresh themselves in. What about freshman English teachers? How spontaneous can they be at ten, eleven, and two o'clock every Monday, Wednesday, and Friday for five, seventeen, thirty-odd years? Maybe there are a few workhorse saints of freshman English, but what about ordinary folk?

If I am not to be convicted of elitism and dreaminess, I must respond to this legitimate objection. The rest of this essay is that response.

II

To begin with, I accept it as a given that most teachers are ordinary folk—always have been, always will be. But I believe that ordinary folk, respectable, a bit timid, decent enough, though they are likely to assume those pedagogic postures which have forever been legitimate butts of satire, do not have to assume them. An alternative to squatting sequestered in the fastness of pedantry is to strive in the classroom to let come into being a fragile community. It is in our nature to make such communities, though of course we can be prevented from doing so both by our own negative wills and by too constricting a system (which it is also in our nature to make). The extraordinary ingredient in making communities is not possessing the power to make them but exercising that power, wanting them enough to risk failure. Our life is so far from nature now, so abstract, and system so obstructs us that many no longer know they have the power of communion, of making even fragile communities, and many have too little hope of exercising that power successfully even to try, even to want to try. The faith must be restored. What can we who are believers but not great prophets do to restore this faith except exercise that power as best we can? "We must love one another, or die," Auden wrote many years ago. Later he changed it to "and die." He was right both ways, but the first time much more profoundly.

I also accept it as a given that mass literacy is here to stay for a while as an American ideal. I don't think much of it as an ideal; so far as I can see, a lot of people seem to have no use, much less desire, for any more literacy than it takes to drive a car or to shop for soap in supermarkets, and I think ladling literacy out to them as we now do is not only wrong in itself, like a dole instead of jobs, but generates in them troubles which do not need to be. However, the ideal of mass literacy flourishes, and so long as it continues to be implemented in the schools, freshman English will continue to be with us in college in one of its many forms, few very good, many very bad. In my experience, the worst as well as the most obvious of its forms is bonehead English—system pure, every response re-hearsed. The best is one in which the students' main homework consists of writing essays to be revised according to the teacher's corrections and the classroom time is spent in literary appreciation or in disussing ideas derived from good texts or in going over a student paper. Students at every level, from grammar school to graduate creative writing courses, learn how to write adequately by writing and rewriting rather than by studying rhetoric as a con-scious discipline. Indeed, the prose which linguists write in their essays makes me doubt whether the power to join words well is in any way connected to the knowledge it takes, say, to distinguish between an ablative absolute and a schwa. A class in which ideas are discussed and papers are written from those discussions may fail, but it is not doomed to the certain death of bonehead English; it has a chance, at least, of coming to life.

Moreover, I believe it is true that teaching freshman English well is important for the good of our society, which, as everybody recog-nizes, is in a perilous condition. In my hierarchy of values, our gravest dangers are less those peculiar to us than those we share with the other great rationalized nations, and very few social ills are greater threats to us now than the degradation of our language. In the article on the fused participle in *Modern English Usage,* the brothers Fowler, those glorious pedants, wrote this: "It is perhaps beyond hope for a generation that regards *upon you giving* as normal English to recover its hold upon the truth that grammar matters. Yet every just man who will abstain from the fused par-ticiple . . . retards the progress of corruption." Let me spell out how seriously I view the corruption of language. If the general support were to be withdrawn simultaneously from medicine till it reverted to leeches, from marriage till it became a euphemism for shacking up, and from money till a cup of coffee cost three million dollars, our society would not suffer more than it will suffer if the mass media are permitted to triumph utterly. McLuhan prophesies, and many agree, that the media must triumph; if I believed that, I would not want to live, I would go get a job in advertising where the pay at least is better than it is in academia, I would certainly not be

writing this essay. Before electronics, illiteracy safeguarded the
language of large populations from the incursions of the media,
and they used their own words, sometimes well; in this age of electronics and mass semi-literacy only a certain sophistication in language among large numbers of citizens can safeguard it. The language of ecstasy is used to sell perfumed toilet paper, words of
passion to name automobiles, the tongue of trust and family intimacy to persuade the oppressed that they want this rich man
instead of that to govern them, the vocabulary of all elevation has
been repeated into triviality, shoots of spontaneous slang are repeated into self-conscious sterility before they can replenish the
body of language with vigorous grafts, the terms of aesthetic judgment have been repeated into a blur, praise is a noisy blur, con-
tumely is a noisy blur, blur reigns. I have heard, though I do not
know, that, much as the media have done to degrade language in
our nation, they have done worse hurt in Russia; there, such opposition as they are pestered by comes mostly from poets, those very
unacknowledged legislators. One of the reasons some vigor of language is still with and of us in the United States is freshman
English, which has been at war against clichés, distortion by in-
nuendo, great vacuous assertions, quicksand logic, against agit-
prop and adspeak, as long as I can remember; and if we do not
succumb finally to some computer-made Esperanto of efficiency,
one of the reasons will be freshman English. An early act of a
stupid totalitarian regime in this country would be to abolish freshman English; an intelligent regime would sanction and accelerate
the conversion of it into bureaucratized business English and call it
"communication skills."

Perhaps I exaggerate. The homogenization of language is my
worst fear next to Nothingness and my worst nightmare. Nightmare
is provided with images not by Nothingness but by the approaches
to it, and of these the unsouling of language is the one that hits me
hardest. But whether I exaggerate the threats to which our language
is subjected and underestimate its power to resist them, surely I do
not exaggerate the pedagogic importance of making an English

class into a little community. In any kind of class, the experience of community is important of itself; but insofar as the purpose of a class is to impart information and skills on the order of geology or auto-repairing, community is obviously not essential as it is in football or chorus. In this respect, language is ambiguous: nowhere can an individual retreat more intimately than into that supreme social creation, and The Word simultaneously joins you to others and brings others into yourself. Learning language by rote from books is to the intercourse of living speech as masturbation is to marriage; and ambiguous marriage itself is an intercourse first of words and then of bodies. Your job as English teacher is to get the students to use language your way in large part as a result of wanting to, not having to, be together with you. The teacher from whom a student learns English best is the one to whom he is most connected, and though personal connection may be the finest, the connection of classroom community is as much as an ordinary English teacher need aspire to; it is enough; it can do the job.

The teacher who stays alive is the one who is always learning something new, about his subject, about students, about teaching itself.

When studying a text in class, let the students know your likes and dislikes, your ignorances, your shortcomings.

Don't make them do their reading by forcing them to take factual tests on the assignments. In fact, don't *make* them do anything; let the system do that; that is what it is needed for.

Commend every spark of imagination they show on paper and in class. The better the student, the more scrupulously you must point out his weaknesses—he won't trust unadulterated praise, for he believes he is flawless no more than you do. Overcorrect only those whom you want to keep from writing, for overcorrection is a form of punishing discouragement and only that.

In formulating topics for themes, exert all the imagination you have; seek counsel from books and colleagues; ask your students to help you.

Curtail the talkative, but not by sarcasm; entice, do not harass, the shy out into the open.

When you have been wrong admit it. When you have hurt a student's feelings, apologize to him. Tell the class ahead of time what constitutes a transgression and how you intend to punish it. When they or you feel like straying from the subject, stray a while. When you feel like smiling, smile. Use your eyebrows, your lips, your hands.

When a session is a bust, dismiss class early, or, if you'll get in trouble for doing that, let the rest of the period be a reading time—if you have any talent for it, read aloud to them. And tell them why you are doing what you are doing: one way to teach students how to communicate is to communicate with them.

Tell them early what you think of having to give grades.

Always hold in mind: much that is old to you is new to them. Speak to their freshness, that your weariness at making a point for the seven hundredth time may not show. This, like a good deal else that goes on in a classroom, is a matter of courtesy.

Know the text at hand far better than what you are going to say about it, even when you are going to repeat what you have said before.

Think of yourself as an actor or rhapsode who must say the same thing over and over, yet each time afresh. You must have a primary faith in the opinions you are uttering, wanting the students to share those opinions or at any rate to consider them seriously, above all to look at the text from which the opinions derive. How to make your utterances sound fresh? Partly by mere technique, but more by not thinking about them between times, by a forced forgetting. Yet, sooner or later, you are likely to hear yourself saying something important not because, not even as though, you mean it at that moment but just because you have said it before: time to change texts.

Words are motions of the air between mouth and ear. Writing makes silent signs for living sounds. It can take on a fine life of its own, but that life is of necessity parasitic on speech. Poetry is a form not of writing but of saying, and the analytic way of teaching it which is dominant in our colleges now is by no means superior to teaching students to read it aloud. To teach English is to present models of ways of talking.

Dickens, that handful of dust, speaks to me; whereas a tepid sack of guts who avidly corrects my spelling errors, ignores my unassigned gropings for words by which to understand the strangenesses I see in the world, and chides my wit for its clumsiness and my lovely phrases for their softness, neither speaks to me nor makes me want to speak. He is not teaching, he is anti-teaching.

Socrates and Jesus, those teachers, seldom said what they meant. Socrates was a great ironist; Jesus used paradox and dazzling nonsense ("the meek shall inherit the earth"); both told good parables, stories which are not exhausted by the morals attached to them. More often than not, if you can say what you mean, you don't mean much.

Don't cheapen irony by using it as a mask for timidity.

To teach writing at every level does not mean to prescribe rules, assign topics, or recommend forms. To teach writing is to help to rewrite. The only point at which I, either as teacher or as writer-friend, can legitimately enter into the work of another, however humble it may be, however exalted, is to suggest ways by which or at least areas in which he might improve it.

The metaphor of writing as organic, a natural, spontaneous expression of the writer himself, has proved to be immensely valuable in criticism; but it does at least as much harm as good for the teaching of writing, for it leaves nothing for the student, much less the teacher, to do once the soil is prepared and the seed planted (and exactly what do those metaphors mean?). It is better to compare a sentence, a paragraph, a whole essay, even a story or poem, to a mechanism with replaceable and movable parts; for in this way revision is thought of less as a tampering with something uniquely the writer's own than as a sort of puzzle which can be assembled in more than one way, but in one way best. Yet the mechanism must seem a living artifice, like one of Yeats's Byzantine hammered gold birds set upon a golden bough.

System.

To teach English well is to conspire within and to some extent against the system that employs you, however good it is. (If it is bad enough, you can hardly work in it at all, even conspiratorially.) For it is in the nature of system to begin to ossify as soon as it takes shape, and as an educational system ossifies, it more and more tells you ahead of time what to say. The only kind of class I know of that approaches bonehead English in dullness is a graduate seminar in which trainee professors are working diligently to learn what to say ahead of time in the classes they will soon teach: they think their jobs depend on it. Such a class would not be dull if only they would concern themselves that seriously with the kind of speech their lives depend on. In fact, not even their jobs depend on dullness as much as they think: the conspiracy is an open one.

I hope that Friedenberg and Co. do not get stuck in the habit of demolition and I especially hope they never get it into their heads that system can be replaced by some non-system, by love. I hope they create and disseminate a strong conception of a good educational system and of how to get there from here. But the moment their system succeeds I shall begin to subvert it. In the classroom at least. Though not wholeheartedly. For as a matter of fact, you can have too little of system, procedure, the law.

One of the reasons I like teaching in the Syracuse English department is that I am not obliged to do any committee work. Being unforced, I have served on several committees willingly, including one to find a new chairman—distillate of system! Moreover, I have helped to institute a new committee (after all, "committee" means "a bringing together") that we needed because of the creative writing program of which I am a part. In this program, we give an M.A. to a student who fulfills the course requirements demanded for a regular scholarly M.A. and who also submits, instead of two expanded and polished seminar papers, a thesis consisting of a novel or a small book of poems or short stories. (A system is not yet ossified which can stretch "thesis" to include, say, a novel on the love and drug lives of far-out college students.) But suppose a candidate's writing is, in our judgment, not of acceptable quality. Who is to tell him so, and when? Nobody wants to, for we may all like him and think him intelligent, just not gifted. If all of us professors in the program were of stern moral fiber, there would be no problem. But we are not. We need a procedure and a committee. We "creative" teachers, egged on in part by shaggy, subversive, anti-system students in whom our lack of procedure was generating unnecessary anxiety, have made a system for ourselves and like it.

A very long time ago in Europe when a thesis was still a thesis, a candidate for a high degree had to stand in a public hall before learned examiners whose peer he hoped to become and defend his thesis against their probing, attaining his degree only if he succeeded orally in protecting that thesis well. The defense of thesis became an established part of the educational system in the West, and we at Syracuse require it of, say, a girl who has written a batch of poems about how she was bugged by her parents and who is she anyhow.

One such defense I sat on (examining professors no longer attack a thesis, they sit on it) was for a young man who had written a novel which we who made up his committee thought well of. By the time this last formality was due, we had already passed him and he knew it. As we examiners ritualistically had him wait outside the door while we conferred, we agreed that we would keep him only half the legal hour. But in fact we stayed the whole time, because we got involved with him in a conversation we were enjoying too much to break up. One of the professors, a critic, was annoyed by a shifty statement in the candidate's required summary of thesis and by his stubborn refusal to modify it. He had written that his purpose in writing his novel had been to tell a good story, and when asked why he had done this, that, or the other thing in the book, he would reply with steadfast shiftiness that he had done it because he thought it would make the story better. He already had a teaching job lined up for the fall. "Well," said the professor in exasperation, "if you were teaching this novel in an English class, what would you say about it?" "Oh, I'd go on about themes and point of view and symbols and that. But they aren't why the guy wrote the story or why I chose it to teach, and I'd let the students know that. Still, you got to keep talking."

My little story is not yet over. In the letter of recommendation I had written for him that spring to send around with job applications, I had mentioned that he, an Alabamian who had served his tour of duty in the Air Force, had been recently active in peace and civil rights demonstrations. One afternoon a month before the defense of thesis, I had received a telephone call from the chairman of the English department of a new Virginia college. This stranger, who identified himself as a retired Air Force officer, said they were considering our candidate and wanted to know more about the political activities I had mentioned in the letter. System had not obliged me to mention his politics; but he and I and the world at large agreed that such activities were an important part of a man, of a teacher, even though not connected with his literary studies or capacities. I told that officer on the other end of the wire the truth of what I knew and my true opinion on it. And I felt somewhat like a betrayer because this student had become something of a friend by now. The next day he dropped by to tell me that the previous evening that same chairman had phoned him, in part because of what I had said about our candidate's politics, to offer him a job, which, partly because they wanted him politics and all, he had accepted.

I guess I'm not absolutely convinced that what we most need is a total revolution of the educational system right this minute. For though at its worst it can outright forbid, and though even at its best it somewhat hinders, the community of classroom, yet our system never commands us to make such a community. Freedom to make or not make a community of a class as you choose is essential if you are to make it at all. Yet much freedom means much responsibility. It is up to each of us to lay himself on the line in every class.

5

Teaching Writing:
A Letter to the Editor

GEORGE GARRETT

Dear Jon,

Sorry about long delay on this piece. No excuse really. Sure, I could honestly claim busyness and business, just like everybody else I know of. Have been busy, it's true, with many things. Among them earning my living. That is, in fact and in flesh, teaching writing. But still that would be faking it. Truth is, I have tried to get this piece on teaching writing going maybe a half a dozen times and failed every time to make it work.

Funny thing. Because, Lord knows, I have plenty of ideas, notions, whims, opinions, and guesses about the subject. And have talked about it here and there in public, and I have even written on the subject a few times. But, as is always the case I think, I wasn't pleased with what I said or wrote at the time I was doing it and am even less so now.

Which is the first tentative point. The whole of Creation is change, constant change. So it is right and proper that those whose lives are engaged, involved, and dedicated to the creation of anything—any *thing*—should also be moving to and living by, in, and with the mysterious energy of the Creation. Which mystery and energy is continually made manifest in the one immutable constant —change.

Anyway, without trying to sound and seem so grand, I can put it another way. I am actually engaged in the odd performing art of teaching. And I have been so for more than a dozen years, off and on. In various places. I play by ear and I improvise as I go along. And, to double the problem of point of view, I am also writing myself at the same time. Doing the thing that I teach. (Though from the beginning I have taught other things too.)

Which adds up to the simple brute fact that anything I have to say about my experience and notions on the subject of teaching writing is bound to be fragmentary, personal, pragmatic, limited by my own strengths and weaknesses. Best I can do is to try to tell it like it seems to be. And there will be some sort of truth in that. Just enough truth so that the whole of it should be viewed with cautious skepticism.

So much has changed. And changed more swiftly than we have the power or the imagination to notice.

Example: the writer as teacher, especially in the colleges and universities. When I was a student, and it doesn't seem *that* long ago, writers on faculties were few and far between. People wrote then, as they do now, about "the place of the writer" in academe. Only then it had more meaning, because there were very few places where a writer had any place. Now the writer has his place in lots of places. Practically every place. I travel around a lot, making a hard-earned buck on the lower echelons of the lecture and reading circuits. So far I have yet to find a school that is so small, poor, remote, and unrenowned as not to have at least *one* writer on the staff. And my writing students are getting jobs, some of them very good jobs and all of them getting easier to get every year, all over the country. This, in itself, is neither good nor bad, promising or foreboding. It's just a fact of life as we live it now. And it is news to nobody I know of except a few Grand Old Men of the Modern Languages Association. Bless their hard hearts.

But it wasn't always so. If writers justly complain from time to time that colleges, and especially English departments, are hostile territory, dangerous turf, they should pause to remember the old-timers, some living and working still, some dead and gone, the pioneers and prospectors who went in a generation or more ago and fought the good fight, got regularly reamed and scalped and racked, but meanwhile fought and won. We, the recent and more comfortable colonists, have it easy. The least we can do is to remember them sometimes with a salute of thanks. Some were writers and some were not. Some taught creative writing openly. Others sneaked it into the curriculum, past daffy deans and dozing department chairmen, camouflaged as Advanced Composition, Studies in Rhetoric, etc. Each of my own generation would have his own list of names based on those he knows and knows of. My own is so limited. But, incomplete as it is and must be, I can nevertheless say flatly that I wouldn't be here nor would most of the contributors, nor would there be very much teaching of creative writing if it had not been for the inimitable likes of Richard Blackmur (Princeton), Jesse Rheder (Chapel Hill), William Blackburn (Duke), Ruth Pennybacker (Houston), George Williams (Rice), A. K. Davis (Virginia), Wallace Stegner (Stanford), Brewster Gheslin (Utah), Louis D. Rubin, Jr. (Johns Hopkins, Hollins, Chapel Hill), John Crowe Ransom (Kenyon), Wilbert Snow (Wesleyan), Andrew Lytle (Florida and Sewanee), Babette Deutsch (Columbia), J. Frank Dobie (Texas), and so many others it would take a fair size directory to name them and a fat book to celebrate their doings. And somebody ought to do that book.

I begin, then, with a backward glance. Saluting some of the originals. Those who are dead, may they rest in peace. Those in retirement, live long and enjoy. Those still out in the sun chopping cotton with the rest of us, conserve yourselves like real professionals, go steady and easy. And please tell us a few of the good things you know.

The Writer in the College

Good things: regular but modest pay, modest enough to keep him writing if only to feed and clothe his kids; good, though irregular hours; good vacations with time to do his own work; plenty of smart people around, the scholars and critics and wheeler-dealers who can teach him a lot if he refuses to take them too seriously; the constant adventure of the young, who can't "keep him young," but can remind him continually that he was young too and even, sometimes, make him glad that he is not young and suffering exactly the same way any more; the young who can also force him to question his hard-earned habits and to try to articulate his simplest assumptions and thus identify them as such before they settle with rigidity into laws and tablets.

Bad things: the academic set of values of art, which, perhaps justly, is most concerned with such things as *reputation* and *influence,* etc.; the academic climate of intense paranoia; the fact that most writing is done in and during vacations, meaning that a whole generation of American writing is being produced in the summer and over Christmas holidays and surely *that* will have some curious imaginative influence; the inevitable growth and flourishing of that ungainly weed, "the academic novel" (or poem, story, play); the young who contribute, yes, but also can make a man feel smarter and wiser than he really is or, conversely, confirm his suspicion that the world is going to hell in a creaky wheelbarrow and "progress" is not in learning but in trying not to forget too much, to stave off the shades of senility; and not to forget that now the writer is *almost* respectable in academe, he has to pay the price for that if he wants it—to "publish or perish" with every other ambitious hack in the teaching trade.

A neutral item: writers-in-residence and visiting writers. These freelance cavaliers come and go, brightly, according to their current rating on the board of the literary stockmarket. And no harm there—except the gut-gnawing and teeth-grinding of simple deadly Envy. Which, after all, can be recognized and named, if not suppressed. But nonetheless much falls upon the Local Man, the teacher, when the Distinguished Visitor is at hand. Some is real, such as services to be rendered. For it is, of course, assumed that (like being the Negro at a party when another walks in) one writer will best know how to handle another. And some, no less real, is less tangible. For example, the *political* considerations. If X comes to visit and snubs you or cuts you dead, it is noted. One's local standing drops. Or the opposite. If Y comes to town and boozes like a trooper and chases cheerleaders and (ever and always) ends up, at best, with a lean myopic lady graduate student or a frigid faculty wife, is a hit or bombs out, somehow *you* are responsible.

The Imagination

Statistically the student of today is smarter than ever before. He knows so many things, does well on tests and such, and it is tougher to get into college than it used to be. Deans of Admissions are forever reminding me and others too that with *our* high school records we would never make it today.

Maybe so. But along with all this academic *finesse,* this light-footed, measurable intellectual agility, go some other interesting and sometimes depressing characteristics.

Obviously one is that the ones who make it are the ones who have figured out how to beat the System and either figured it is worth beating or not worth not beating. No wonder they rage and rave against the System, even though, superficially, it has been good to them. Having sold out somewhere around the Seventh Grade, having learned to be Operators early, they are (as we all are) most at war with themselves, most apt to detect their own vices in others.

No harm in that. Within reason they are fairly hard to con these days.

But with all their demonstrable knowledge, do they *know* anything more? I mean know in the Biblical sense, copulation, *carnal knowledge,* involving the mystical intercourse of thought, feeling, and imagination.

I think not. I think they know less, really. They can shuffle and deal abstractions like a Mississippi riverboat gambler. They can draw, *fast* draw a generalization quicker than Wyatt Earp could draw and fan his .44. But—witness their own complaint, the complaint of the best of them—in feeling, in imagination, they are cripples. Cripples who want urgently, eagerly, to join in the dance which is life. But they don't know how. Somebody forgot to teach them.

Today's students, more than ever before (and I include all the human history I know of) desperately need the repair work of working with their five senses, their feelings, the imagination. They need all the arts. Need to *practice* these arts, with or without "talent."

Thus writing, whether or not it results in the encouragement of one real and true writer, is a vital part of education today. I think everybody in school should at least have a chance to try it.

Especially those who have been exposed to a heavy dose of formal courses in Literature. Every year the critics get younger and smarter. This is because contemporary literary criticism is farther and farther removed from the practice and process of making. Often from real life itself, never mind art. It has become increasingly formalized, riddled with habits and jargon. Both easy enough for a bright kid to pick up without knowing why or what for. Or even caring.

One value of doing some writing, clumsy as it may be, is to come to appreciate what a masterpiece (commonplace enough in the rigid context of curriculum) really is, *why* it is masterful. To learn that to write even the simplest things well requires craft and skill and commitment they have not been told to notice and admire. To see and feel that even "trash" is, like the Sweet Singer of Michigan said about "the Literary," "very difficult to do."

There's a great deal of value in the *unlearning* of clichés and bad habits. Generalization of my own: "All serious students of literature should take creative writing. At least they might acquire a measure of common humility."

But the acquisition of inhibitions, even more or less virtuous ones, is not a giant step toward wisdom. One must learn to overcome many inhibitions as well. Whether they have been acquired or merely drummed into the mind and spirit. Here, paradoxically, the making of things, the practice and process of creation, can help enormously to liberate.

Example: It does no harm to learn that some "masterpieces" are not entirely the result of craft, even "trash" being sometimes more crafty, but come from what was well called "the grace beyond the reach of art."

The discipline of writing can create its own hungers and needs. These new and previously unimaginable lusts can be most energizing and invigorating, if not inspiring.

But, Jon, you think (I can imagine you thinking) I am dodging the issue and the subject like a rodeo clown jump-down in a barrel. I mean, here I am and I still haven't gotten around to the How To Do It part.

Of course, there are *reasons*. The best one being that I don't have *a* way, a method of teaching writing. No fixed method except to admit that I haven't got one. Which, as a pedagogical habit, can become as much a method as any other. And I distrust pedagogical habits, especially my own.

Safer, and fortunately more accurate, to say that I have no one fixed working method, but make use of many.

I am familiar with the advantages and disadvantages of most of the methods writers, as teachers of writing, use. The most appreciable advantage of almost any fixed method, one much appreciated, by the way, by today's students, is that those who can thrive under and against the demarcations of a clearly defined discipline tend to do very well indeed. Not only (though this is a matter of utmost importance to the student at the time) as students in a course, but also as writers. And once the rules of the game are known, as they can be soon enough and easy enough in such a case, those who do not choose to play that game or by those rules can avoid the whole experience by free rational choice.

I am *not* so certain of my critical or technical assumptions as I am of the assumption that it is not necessarily the chief purpose and function of a writing course to "produce" writers. A fair number, growing as the years add up, of my students, of varying degrees of talent, of differing gifts, have managed to see their work published. Others have not. What this means, I am not sure.

I am not at all sure, either, whether what might be attributed to one man's system or another's is not in truth more the effect of the man himself, in the ancient and honorable role of influence and example, than of whatever system he works with or by. To deny or even to underestimate the influence of example, of the human, in the arts seems to me the most crude sort of folly. A good teacher can transcend any system, even his own. A bad teacher will do small good no matter how excellent the virtues of his method.

I can say this and not without a little strut of pride: that none of my students who have gone on to be writers of one kind or another write like me. That they do not write like each other. A good many do not even like each other. Which is, for me, as it should be.

The Aim of the Course

Purposes are not the same, depend upon point of view. The institution offers the course in competition with other institutions, because it has to. Proposes to give time and full credit for the learning and practice of an art. Also as a kind of inexpensive group therapy. And with the very vague general hope that somebody, someday, somehow, who has taken the course will write something which will be celebrated and maybe win some kind of a prize and, thus, reflect well and publicly upon the institution. The powers that be are too worldly-wise to count on this; the odds are bad. But in the event it should happen, they are fully prepared to make the most of it. Also, having such courses gives them something to do with the writer or writers they employ.

Purpose of the student. Who knows? God knows. They sign up. Some want to write. Some just want to take the course. When there are interviews they generally fall into two categories: those who say they want to write and those who say they want *to see if they can write.* By all good reasons the latter should be eliminated at the outset. Writing is not something you can take a course in to see if you can do. Further, the attitude indicates not only a lack of even rudimentary knowledge of the art and craft, but also a casual window-shopping approach to life at best. But the latter also has the advantage, not inconsiderable, of pure innocence. Rare among today's students. The former could just as well be shrewd experience. It is difficult to guess the truth. Best not to try.

Talent is sometimes a test, one way or another. The submission of some manuscripts for example. But there are many variables here. And, as one who has been involved in athletics both as a player and a coach, I know by heart too many examples of athletes blessed with all the equipment nature can lavish who nevertheless were not much good. And can cite an equal number of examples of those who had everything going against them except desire, will, and eventually, some luck.

Neither talent nor intelligence can make a good writer. I know quite a few good writers who have not much of either.

Back to the students. One cannot know *their* impulses and reasons for studying writing. One can remember well enough, therefore imagine without strain, their point of view. They may or may not have a teleology, but for certain they are living in a strictly limited context. Within that context they want to graduate. To graduate they want to take courses which will not be too risky, will permit them the best chance for an easy good grade. Let the goal of wisdom take care of itself. The urgent item on the agenda is survival. In an entirely secondary sense there is a modest prestige in certain circles these days, good report and repute at simply being an aspiring young writer. Will take a man far. All the way through youth in fact. Which may be a mild motivation.

The writer-teacher? He wants to keep his job, therefore must do it. Like everyone else, he wants to improve his position and status; therefore he must do it well, as well as he can. Must therefore seek to satisfy both students and higher powers without a serious diminution of his own powers of self-esteem.

A thoroughly human drama it is, then. Properly predicated upon the conflict and conformity of self-interest. Changed slightly, though, sometimes even saved from destructive self-interest, by the truth that writing is an art and teaching is an art. And all the arts partake of mystery and magic. Magic of transformation.

In the end, often, in fact frequently, students, teacher and sometimes even the hierarchical powers forget *why* they are so engaged.
At which point original motivations are without any meaning.

My General Aim

As it has developed, my aim is to be a *constructive* critic.

By constructive criticism I mean that it is my role and duty to be
a sympathetic critic, insofar as possible, in several important ways.
I shall not question either the practicality of the student's aim or,
in general, his means. Shall question and seek to find some answers,
ways to help him realize his aims within the limits of his means and
the terms of his rules. If he wants to write an epic poem, fine. If
the student wishes to write and *publish* an epic poem in this day
and age, that's another problem.

I neither encourage nor discourage publication. Those who seek
to be published are encouraged in every way I know how, but as
honestly as I can, with a minimum of false hopes and illusions.
Those who write what is clearly publishable or seems to be *intended* for publication, but who profess to be above such mundane
matters, are gently reminded in several ways that in their own terms
the tedious trivialities of submission and rejection or acceptance
are a matter of final commitment and honesty.

Obviously it is a highly personal, individual thing, this part of
my teaching. The main burden of it is, then, alone, in tutorial
conference.

What of the classroom, since there must be (usually) some
meeting of the group?

The easiest, most common, and most tempting method is to
devote the meetings to the discussion and criticism of student
manuscripts. Or, lacking those, to turn the course into yet another
session of literary criticism. The latter they tend to enjoy, being far
more sure of themselves as critics than makers.

I have found that there are dangers in making a program out of
either method. Groups, though each is always different, tend rapidly

to develop a character and cliques and hierarchical orders. All
writers want and respond to an audience. The result of the over-
organized practice of group criticism seems to me to create an
audience and performers for that particular audience. They write
in terms of that audience, for or against it, to please or to outrage
it, to win the favor or gain the attention of the teacher.

Thus my plan. (It can hardly be called a method.) No student
at any time to be *required* to present work to the group. A free and
voluntary submission instead. Which may be duplicated and read
in advance or in class, anonymously or under the proper name of
the writer. Or may be read aloud, again anonymously or not, by
the teacher or the author or anyone else. All these decisions are left
to the student. A very educational experience. The students of this
liberated generation hate to make decisions. They prefer to counter-
punch. What they don't know is that a counterpuncher is, unless
very quick and crafty, wildly vulnerable. A counterpuncher most
of the time has to trade licks, to get hit in order to hit back. There
is no sport in counterpunching a punching bag.

And there is a standing agreement that the student who wishes
to try work and gain a reaction of the group may volunteer to do so
at any time. That is, it may be planned well in advance or, by the
same rule, may happen *during* the class. Provided another student's
work is not interrupted. My talking and teaching may be interrupted at any time for this purpose.

The exceptions to the general rule are "class assignments," that
is exercises, usually as zany and mind-bending as possible, designed
and controlled so as to spare the exposure of the naked and raw ego.
By the same token, designed, hopefully and covertly, to loosen up
the kinks and muscles and sometimes to prove something about the
craft of writing.

These exercises have included a little of everything and are
almost too silly to mention: from the making of *collage* to writing
letters to Walter Cronkite, these written by an old lady who
assumed (as not a few old folks do) that if she could see Walter,
he could see her; from writing captions for cartoons and advertise-
ments to the most ambitious, the rewriting and "updating" the

Second Book of Spenser's *Faerie Queene* in the inimitable style of Tom Wolfe. Out of one classroom exercise came an anthology that was published (and rapidly remaindered): *The Girl in the Black Raincoat*. Where the work of students was placed side by side with some very well-known writers—poets like Donald Justice, William Jay Smith, Babette Deutsch, Barbara Howes, etc.; novelists like Robie Macauley, William Manchester, David Slavitt, Mary Lee Settle, and Leslie Fiedler. I suppose I should feel sorry for the publisher in his hasty necessity to turn a book into pulp. But, then, any publisher unable to make *some* mileage out of the mere simultaneous presence of, say, Fiedler, Slavitt, and Manchester, each with an original story written for the volume, ought to be in the pulp business. Most interesting thing was this, though. Except in New York, where reviewers were cagey but shrewdly suspicious, careful lest it was an anti-anthology (which, of course, it was), the writers, students, and old pros alike were treated as equals (which, in this context, they were) in the reviews that poured in from all over the country. And, best of all as a teaching device, sooner or later every single writer in the book was cited by someone somewhere as "the best" writer in the book.

Meanwhile a thread of teaching goes along. Writing as art, craft, and business.

The art of it can't be so much taught or learned as demonstrated. When we teach the art of writing we return to essentials—to "show and tell." For craft we look at anything written, from matchcovers to full-length works and including any form that uses words. Opera, for example, or the movies. All are treated with equal seriousness and equal disinterest. We leave the superiority of one form over another or one work over another to the Literature classes.

It follows that a large part of my effort is to brush away cobwebs and clichés. To unlearn as much as we learn. To make the course of study as different and distinct as possible from the conventional courses. It follows that we make not a great deal of the differences in forms and *genres*, looking instead in all things for common characteristics. Ever seeking to create our own taxonomy and to see how it works.

I have said "our" and "we," because I consider myself, as much as I can be realistically, a participant rather than an observer. Learning myself as we go along together.

It follows also that in the name of craft we try to question everything, all the current critical assumptions and fashions. Without awe or reverence. The good ones can stand the strain. The weak ones don't deserve to.

You can call this anarchy if you please. I'd still prefer to think of it as improvisation.

Business

If possible, I try by outside reading assignments, by classroom work, and through occasional visitors to inform my students of what can be told and so seldom is: the rules and rituals, follies and fallacies, aims and failures, of the American literary scene; how and why and by whom magazines and publishing houses are run; what values to place upon professional editorial or critical response. They soon realize, on their own, that judging by the evidence, publishing is a badly run sort of business; that there are precious few editors like the late Saxe Commins or the late Maxwell Perkins; that publishing, at all levels, is supposed to be a profit-making business and that because it is a badly run business it does not turn much profit and publishers are reduced to a kind of gambling that would make any self-respecting gambler blush for shame and plead insanity; that "quality" has very little to do with anything even assuming that someone could recognize it if it bit him like a snake; that therefore they are liberated, free to write what they please perhaps as never before, for, the odds being what they are and the situation being as it is (and only Success can spoil this), it doesn't make very much difference what they write; finally that there is no value in trying to anticipate or second-guess a contemporary American publisher. Jon, would you seriously try to second-guess a man who would bet all his chips on double-O at the roulette wheel? Pray for him, maybe, especially if some of those

chips represent *your* time, energy, hard labor. But it would be
easier to guess the motivations of the Boston Strangler than to try
to figure the rationale of American publishing. And it's good to
know this early.

A good exercise, a healthy one, for example, is to take the year
1920 as a beginning and, with each student taking a different
year and reporting on it, to learn what books were most successful
or celebrated, most widely reviewed or largely ignored, the prize
winners and prize losers. Then to compare the view of the year
itself with our current picture of the same period.

This can be rather entertaining. Take a look at 1929 sometime.
Not a shameful year at all, rather typical. A vintage year, though,
for fine books ignored or misread while other books (and their
critics), much discussed, have since been dutifully forgotten.

Anyway, a certain skepticism about such matters as reputation,
influence, etc., here and now and not in the seventeenth century,
can help a writer to live a little easier in the world he has to live
in. Can help the reader to trust himself a bit more, becoming at
least less likely to be manipulated by the managers, salesmen,
operators, etc. Can offer transferable values to the serious student
who may become a good critic or scholar. For instance, it is just
possible that as a scholar he may recognize that the prevailing
"climate of opinion" about any given writer or period in the past
is as much a function of our times and our assumptions as the
current ratings on the literary stockmarket. And the young critic
may see the same thing and see no reason, except for the common
political and practical reasons, not to be an adventurer. Need not
always stand in line waiting for the hints and clues of the masters
and his betters. May strike out and make a "discovery" or two of
his own. And none need be complete victims of the star system,
reading only the "right" things.

Pretty disruptive things going on in my class, Jon. A handful of
sassy and irreverent anarchists coming along each year. Which
would be true enough, I suppose, if I were a real influence upon
any of these young people. But, don't you see? when the shedding

of inhibitions and the celebration of human freedom are the primary aim, I, the teacher and thus Mr. Inhibition in person, must either be expendable or else be a hypocrite. Better the former. It's not so bad. It is a seasonal thing, anyway. Like some of the ancient gods, I die once an academic year only to rise again for the next one.

The real danger to me, as writer, is more subtle. Teaching is an art, an eminently satisfactory form. And has advantages over the lonesome craft of the writer, chasing little words across a blank page. My problem. My sack of rocks, to be sure. So far I haven't sweated it too much. Have, in academe, had it good and had it bad. Have met some of the finest men I've ever known this side of the Field Artillery. And on at least one occasion worked for a man so wicked, spiteful, and small of spirit that it took me years to begin to imagine what my senses and my mind kept telling me. The best thing about this experience was to learn to subject imagination to the influence of mind and senses. Blatant wickedness (I do not, of course, speak of sin or evil, which are more subtle) is not so rare as it is camouflaged, even from the wicked, these days. Of course the Psalmist's lament—"Why do the ways of the wicked prosper?"—remains terrifyingly pertinent and unanswerable. All the more so when the wicked are assured that their actions, behind a smile, are performed in the name of some good. But my man, the one who taught me to take a lot of long-dead men, Machiavelli for example, with new seriousness, my tutor in the simply wicked, was as clear-cut a case as Crabby Appleton on *Tom Terrific*. I owe him a lot in that sense. I could have lived a whole lifetime in invincible ignorance without his brisk and unsentimental course in the art of ruthless double-dealing.

All very educational, both ways. Becoming a teacher, I did not take the road less traveled by. Took an ordinary road, if a *little* off the beaten track. And, ever a drifter, I didn't even choose. Just drifted along and here I am.

Everything has to end sometime, even a letter. So, Jon, I'll say to you what is meant for that imaginary reader (and even your probably scowling editor, grease pencil in hand, ready to make all kinds of "improvements"): Stay well. Stay loose. Enjoy. Delight is the beginning of instruction. And the end of instruction is supposed to be wisdom. Which, in turn, is reported by some who ought to know to be more precious than anything else in the world. No doubt that it's the *rarest* thing in this world.

Solemnity and senility will get the best of us yet. Meanwhile, awaiting that day, I suggest you think on the words a student of mine, James Seay, saw painted on a battered old bus, being driven by a double-clutching revival preacher. And Jim Seay wrote a poem about it, a good one, published it, and dedicated it to me. (You see, there are nice things about being a teacher. Sometimes, like this one, you can sneak into a magazine that wouldn't touch your own work with a laser beam.) The words were simple and crudely lettered: "LET NOT YOUR HART BE TRUBLE."

I keep a photograph of that bus, a photo the poet took and sent me, handy.

I recommend that you and that imaginary reader and the troubled editor do the same.

Will furnish copy of photo upon request.

All best wishes—

Sincerely,

George

P.S. I forgot the usual question. *Question:* Can writing be taught? *Answer:* Yes. The only writers I know of who say it can't are, ironically, the most conventional, the ones easiest to imitate since they imitate each other. You can teach almost anyone to write like they do, if you think it's worth the effort.

P.P.S. *Trends.* I forgot about how everyone is interested in trends and "new directions." Do I discern any? Yes, I do. Two, and make of them what you will. (1) The very best and most gifted of the new and youngest writers are writing poems and short stories. Will probably get around to novels sooner or later. Since practically nobody is interested in publishing either poems or short stories, preferring instead to lose money on first novels, the publisher who wanted to grab up a whole generation of American writers is the one who would break the pattern. Start publishing what they are writing now instead of settling for the second string. Most of whom are unlikely to repay the initial investment anyway.

(2) The most exciting of the youngest writers have managed, by needing it desperately, to rediscover the power of the imagination. Their work is free-wheeling, fancy-free, and joyously delightful. And don't cite Barth and Barthelme (both good writers my age) as exemplary "influences." Any resemblance is purely superficial. They don't dig either one in excess. They like Barth best because he professes to dig Borges. And, yes sir, they dig Borges. But these flower children of the imagination are mostly on their own. As aforenoted, things have a way of changing. Things change and the dance goes on.

G.

6

Look Ma, I'm Teaching

IVAN GOLD

Her second or third week back she came up one night to sit in on my class. The suggestion had been mine. She still had no friends in New York, or none I cared to contemplate, but apart from this urge to fill in and supervise her idle hours, I wanted her there to see me work, see Jason work, bestow encomiums, level accusations, consider me credentialized, consider me fraudulent, share the unique experience of J. Sams of all the costive people exhorting others to get off the pot, and by the end of it to judge me as I judged myself, harshly and kindly. We were not able to travel to the U. together. I went to see Frank late that afternoon, in response to his summons of the morning; it was not a scheduled session, but he had taken to using me as his utility man, phoning and trying to fit me in when someone canceled out, to plug and tidy up his working day. Rather than resent it, then, I tried to see it as a tribute to my flexibility and leisure. Considering how little and how irregularly I worked, how I was always teetering on the verge, it would have been mere bitchery to say no. And it would have risked tampering with his affection. (I assumed, after close to three years, that he looked upon me kindly. It was hard to see how else he could have borne it. That he felt or expressed nothing stronger than affection suited me as well. It might even—I gave him all the

credit due him, perhaps a little more—have been part of the
Treatment. I wasn't quite ready for love, or not in that context,
and if *I* knew it, surely he knew it too.) I would not, to tell the
truth, have minded regular hours, rigid, predictable times, like any
run of the mill nine-to-five neurotic, but since this was not in the
cards I strove to make a virtue of uncertainty, to feel one-up and
close to cured if he could come to me for a favor. Some days I was
less successful than on others—days on which I felt much more
a petitioner than a colleague. Anyway, around two, I gave Christa
over-explicit instructions on how to reach the university, together
with a campus map, and departed. I had precious little to tell the
gray man that afternoon. I remembered no dreams. My real life
with my real girl, unlike the ten-year parade of sick dalliance
preceding, which we'd explored to its depths, was in a real way
none of his business, which made large inroads in the things we
had to talk about. Nor did I care to dwell for very much longer on
how difficult it still remained to write fiction for the ages; I had
been sounding that haughty, whining note since the week we began,
and not much had improved or altered in that time. I was beginning
to think, I blurted, that there might not be that much left that he
could do for me. There was a silence. Lying down, this time, I
craned back for a look. He was writing. He looked up. He seemed
unperturbed. Um, well, yes, he agreed we had reached a plateau.
For his part he was content to wait it out, doodle away a fifty-
minute hour or two, gird for the next upward climb. Could we
speed things up? I asked him. I was financially equipped to come
three times a week. I was even eager. In his opinion it wouldn't
help. The material had its own rhythm, emerged in its own sweet
time. For me, twice a week was enough. Disappointed, I calculated
how much money I would save over a year, and made my peace.
(Later I would learn from either Dino or Bob Kane that Covington
once confessed he saw *nobody* more than two times a week, that
it was all he felt he could stand, or handle.) That day I leaped from
the couch and fled the office gladly, trying to metamorphose as
I went, analysand to pedagogue, one madcap role to another.
I caught the Forty-ninth Street crosstown bus on Lexington Avenue

and inched toward the Seventh Avenue subway, past the Waldorf-Astoria, the unlikely supermarket on the corner of Park, past Rockefeller Plaza, the jerkoff cinema between Sixth Avenue and Broadway (a block I would get to know a lot better later on) dined on good greasy hamburgers in some standup Broadway joint, chased by the cardboard coffee a New Yorker or a ballfan comes to love, and descended into the rushhour. I found a seat and I looked through a ms. or two on the way up, things I would be reading to the class that evening, and took renewed pleasure in my own red-inked comments, not all of which I remembered delivering; all were terse, sometimes harsh, more often gentle. By the time I got off at my stop and climbed to my semi-private cubicle on the second floor, nodding to the departmental secretary on the way by, the new hat was fairly well in place.

I had been teaching this, Beginning Fiction, for close to two years. The classes met one night a week. They contained from six to fifteen souls, of all sexes and ages and degrees of mastery of the language, of varying motives and schooling and ambition. I was the sole arbiter of who was qualified to take the course, and I barred no one. Almost always there were two or three sufficiently vocal or productive to get us through the time, and usually there was one, at least, who wrote well enough to keep me interested. But I tried to shortchange no one, in class or in the conference hour. I labored as mightily with the poor spellers and those in-nocent of grammar as with the burgeoning talents, tutor in grade school English one moment, Max Perkins the next, and getting my kicks in both places, but more deeply involved with the urge to discover and guide. Anyone with a story to tell and some glimmer-ing of how to tell it was able to engage me. I have a letter of thanks from a sixty-year-old woman who dealt in Florida real estate, with whose gelid but single-minded prose I took some pains, and there's many a fine young laddie down the years (to count them also since) who's sprouted fuzz on his face from one week to the next in gratitude and emulation; but I was waiting for a darkling virgin-whore, with long black silken hair and fineboned face and a surgeon's nasty talent, who told it from her own deep, liquid

places like it was; I'd give her a quick A+ and bundle her home
and plant her at my desk and be quite stern about her working
hours; and playing hours; I'd badger and coddle her muscular
muse; I'd *be* the bloody thing. Nothing along these lines ever turned
up, though there were damsels who were pretty, others who could
write, and once in a great while some sort of combination; and
one ambitious screwed-up twat from Scarsdale, whose prose was
bitchy-lyrical, who boasted of daddy's wealth and could outdrink
me, who never wore underpants and was accident prone. I allowed
to have her way with me for a couple of rueful weeks near one
semester's end. (She pulled a B−, like the rest.) I mean by the
above no more than that I took these classes seriously, which may
have made me unique in the department. I granted each and every
student, from the opening bell and throughout the term, a suc-
cession of private audiences. These were listed in the catalogue as
"conferences," and were technically part of the course, but most
of my confreres cut them down or out at the earliest pretext, which
saved them the pre-class hour. Not me. I enjoyed lolling in that
three-sided box, at that oversize desk, bright, inlaid light blasting
from the cork ceiling, my name typed neatly on an index card
amidst others more illustrious (we shared the office, rarely met),
the buzz of genuine academics, hog-tied by tenure, from the
cubicles around me, exchanging occasional pleasantries with the
tiny brown woman in the office behind, who taught Swahili, savor-
ing the junk academic mail (sometimes addressed, which raised
some discomfort, to "Professor" Sams), but all of this consumed a
quarter-hour or so, and then I wanted company. So I would
schedule meetings with my students whether or not they wished
them, whether or not they had produced anything about which
they cared to confer. I don't think they minded. Hell, I was cre-
dentializing them, as well as myself. And some of my motives were
less questionable than the rest: I wanted them laboring, and I
wanted to know who they were. I was being paid a certain amount,
around thirty dollars an hour, to tell them something, they were
being charged an exorbitant tuition to find out what it was, and I
meant to impart it. Elusive as it was, it required a certain number

of face-to-face confrontations, and more friendliness and wit than
fire and exhortations. In some of these meetings I learned to understand a little better how a man could turn to lay analysis as a
profession, if he was not too messed up in his own heart of hearts
and lacked all other talents. Within the given range, I was not
equipped too badly. For one thing, I knew firsthand how naked and
spreadeagled the ego can feel when it lays itself out on the page.
I'd taken such courses as an undergrad myself, had been intelli-
gently handled, and tried to pass on what I'd learned. Let me
apologize forthwith to my co-workers of the time who were at least
as noble as I. As for the rest . . . they knew that "teaching writing"
was a con game and that the chief pedagogical challenge was to
keep this knowledge from the marks. Prime example was Mr. Blank,
who headed up the show, but still had to teach a class or two himself. A nondescript and ageless hornrimmed little man from Oregon.
He had a thousand ways to get through the time, a shitsack full of
ploys, and was delighted to share them. You had them grind out
an autobiographical fragment. You assigned them a character
sketch. You asked them for a snatch or two of dialogue. Are they
totally uninspired, duller than dull? Bring in a lively clipping from
the public prints on which they can embroider. If really uptight—
you have some writer friends?—bail out with a guest lecture. He
would fairly chortle as he passed on this wisdom. All of it predicated on the student being a *shmuck*, if only for enrolling in such
an obvious hype in the first place. And yet the man had got to
where he was, occupied his safe, officious niche . . . perhaps he
had an abundance of administrative skills. He frightened me to
death. He had published a work of fiction twenty years before, held
a B.A. in English from his native state. There before my eyes was
the fate of the one-book man with no advanced degrees, clinging
to the outskirts of academe (and livelihood!) by his fingernails, no
longer even dreaming on past glory, not even toting the yellowing
reviews, but all his energies devoted now to fending off the moment
when some wiseass would rise slowly from his place at the seminar
table, on the heels of some hoary, rote pronunciamento ("The thing
you have to remember is, write about what you know." "The

trouble is, your dialogue has no life."), and drawl, "But Mr. Blank,
with all due respect, just what the fuck have *you* written *lately?*"—
but this may not have been his problem, or not any longer, as it
had not yet come to be mine. And all being said, the man had in
him something sensitive, to pain, if not to wit, or maybe both . . .
but to hell with that. Let him mouth his own praises. I just recently
discovered that the son of a bitch had always underpaid me. Crying
poormouth, budgets beyond his control, hostile trustees, but other
writers of no greater merit, if all somewhat older, were receiving
more than I. I suspected it even then, while I still held the job, but
didn't want to check it out, risk the choler I knew I would feel and
so jeopardize the fringe benefits, intangible and other. And there
were others: cheap summer charter flights to foreign places, including the pre-Christa one I signed up for, in December of '64,
loving the bargain, but canceled gladly when the chance arose;
the magnificent library facilities I so rarely used; discounts in the
book stores; signing regally for drinks at the faculty club; but most
important probably the image of myself, as I moved salaried and
purposeful one night a week across the face of alma mater, the
landscaped, improved, but still terribly familiar campus, with
power, a role, an office hour. How different from the jangled ex-GI
with mother's money in his pocket ("Professor" Sams!), up there to
fulfill her destiny; so wonderfully remote from the pimpled loner,
unloved undergrad, eyeing with hostile, hopeless lust the multiform
lovelies who walked those parts, not one of whom in four long years
he ever met, and who had not changed that much in the fifteen
years since, or only in their morals—their young, emancipated
pussies winked and nodded as I passed benignly by, almost
smiling through my beard, writer, mentor, possible lover—these
were the very good moments. At times, especially in colder weather,
I would have to induce them, say a beer or three, or something
more, to ward off a deeper vision, of how little I had really altered
since the beanie days, of how many more or less sophisticated ways
remained until the grave of playing pocket pool. Some weak-
chinned, pockmarked, foureyed, unformed, undergraduate face
might set it off, some terrified cynic-in-training, some spectral

sibling, or maybe just a poor day at the machine, or never getting there at all; and now I was supposed to comment wisely on the work of my charges, or worse yet try to extract it from them, deal firmly with excuses about job pressures, domestic strife, examinations, or the brainbreaking loneliness of the work itself, point up the need for habit, the importance of sitting one's ass at regular intervals before the blank sheet of paper . . . what kind of specialized fraud was I about to become? A boilermaker might do some good on an evening such as that. And if they smelled it on my breath, well that could be twisted, too, should any have the effrontery to call me on it. Brendhan Behan. Dylan Thomas. Lowry. F. Scott. Papa himself. All reasonably prolific, brilliantly dead, all noted for the sauce. So long as I remained coherent, made the occasional coruscating, helpful judgment, none had reason to complain. Nor did anyone, so far as I know.

I had two people due in that night, but neither showed. Zabb, a Jewish schoolteacher from Queens who wrote of how it felt to be a poor southern Negro in the forties, a reasonably skillful (if hard to fathom) imitation of Richard Wright, phoned to say that his wife was ill and he could not make the class, and Delgado, who did come to class, explained that he had been too busy writing his new piece to want to come in and talk about the last. On this night, I didn't mind the solitude. Leaning back, hands behind my head, I sat pondering my book—there was, indeed, a book: I'd enlarged it by a page or so that morning; the thing was sneaking toward completion, phrase by phrase, despite my tears, my spastic efforts to oppose it—and recalling things about my lady. Of how she might come in from her wanderings late of an afternoon, and if the mood was on me I would ask her, "Any adventures?" not really needing to know, and if the mood was on her she would say, why, yes . . . as she was climbing the crud and debris down by Twentieth Street and the East River, making that nearby stench-pond serve her need for open spaces, a tug saluted her in passing, the crew waved and cheered, the boat bellowed again, she finally acknowledged, and she flushed again relating it as she must have at the time, enjoying this present moment, eked out by shrugs and smiles, almost as much as the first, and I struggled to savor it with her, for what sane man is threatened by a tugboat, that many yards from the shore? Yet bugged that all the "adventures" she chose to describe were of this nature (but had I truly meant some other kind?), and soothed on top of that, that if she needed this sort of thing, at least she brought the stories home, laid the world's sexual applause at Poppa's feet, who alone of its vast population, he more or less believed, had real access to the wares. Sometimes she would say nothing about where she had been or what she had done, and that was her privilege, too. Just as it was mine at such moments—for if I had not been really curious to begin with, her silence made me so—to be miffed by her evasive ways.

At twenty minutes past six I began the slow walk to the classroom, on the other end of campus. It was moving toward dusk and the subway heaved out a new academic shift, mostly adults, the "night folk," as we tended to dismiss them, in my snotnosed salad days. A group of college men, great-thighed in shorts, jogged on past, so much athletic meat, giving off their jockstrap aroma even in the open air. Good luck to them, I gave them room. Watching the gladiators on the tube was one thing, imbibing them another. For a while I had a second-string back in my class, a good-natured Pole who turned in one piece early on, a spare account of the pre-game locker room atmosphere, tapings, tensions, friendships strained, which accomplished all that he intended. For Wdowka, too, I had ambitions. I would bring him on slowly, encourage his bent, for no writer had yet come along, so far as I knew, who could carry John R. Tunis' glove. (But a week or so later, pleading academic and gridiron pressures, he dropped the course.) He was one of three people in the room when I arrived. Mrs. Baldakian and Mrs. Hale were the others. Mrs. Hale was my writer; I would be a bit surprised if she has not, by now, achieved some public success. I'd already asked her what the devil she was doing there, in my class or any other, and she replied that she still needed the incentive and the praise. She was in her mid-twenties, thin and tall, a sort of desiccated Jane Mason, drier skin, stringier hair. Once, after class I let her buy me a couple of beers in the local and afterward I walked her home, as I understood it—she led me down a side street to the parapet overlooking the Hudson River, pleasant and deserted, where the warm breeze blew us together and it developed she lived nowhere near. Ah, well. How many can you trust? She had a huge respect for published writers, of which I did not attempt to disabuse her, but explained my domestic situation, gave her a brotherly kiss, and she walked me back to the subway. Her fiction dealt with things like unconsummated dykey affairs and France, and because of the latter preoccupation I slipped up frequently on place-names, but made even more egregious blunders, for she also used English words, always correctly, which I had never seen before. I offered to let her read her own work, but she said she preferred things as they were. Not that she was shy, especially, she simply liked to listen.

A few more arrived, seven of a possible ten, and just before the last, the slightly tardy Delgado, came Christa. She'd put her hair up since I saw her last. She wore her black coat, her patched-up boots. She had to pass me on the way in, my perch at the head of the table, and jutted her underlip in greeting. She paused an instant; I gestured self-consciously toward the several empty chairs, some close at hand. But she took one to the rear, set back a bit from the table. Establishing her distance. Very well. I didn't trouble to inform the class there was a guest in their midst; I doubted she would appreciate it, and they could see it well enough.

After some opening patter, I set up conferences for the following week, and collected what work they had done between the previous week and this. I alerted them to my book review, which was due out the following Sunday. This was hardly the place for false modesty. I turned over the floor for a moment. A girl just out of college was having her problems with "structure" . . . looking wise, I let them kick it around amongst themselves. It wasn't my long suit. Between them, my intellectual and my athlete sorted her out. We were ready to begin. I had brought along a cup of canteen coffee, and so had several others. The atmosphere was relaxed. I was feeling fairly good in any case, sober as a judge and filled with a sense of all our possibilities, but I'd come in with only two things

worth reading aloud over the two hours, works by Baldakian and
Hale, neither awfully long, which could have left us with a sticky
swath of time to fill, but Delgado bailed me out, as (if he showed
up) I had known he would, with another of his chaotic longhand
installments which he had finished, he said, explaining his lateness,
about thirty seconds before, in the john, the subway, a phone
booth, I forget. I believed the dark young handsome skinny bastard
when he said he did his writing everywhere, and he was equally
credible when he said he had never rewritten anything in his life.
He was not against rewrite, he agreed in our meetings that his
work would probably profit by it, but the new material came
gushing at such a rapid rate, what with seeking menial jobs, and
getting jobs, and losing jobs, and getting laid, and not getting laid,
and fighting off queers, and using queers, and getting it all down
while it was fresh, that he had trouble enough keeping pace as it
was. He was about twenty-one, Brooklyn-born, half-Portuguese.
Apart from this, I learned almost nothing about his past; his life
began the day he enrolled in my course. What he was attempting
was nothing less than getting it all down, the ultimate diary, the
tape-recorder-in-the-head, and damned if he wasn't bringing it off
to an impressive degree. Of course some process of selection was
at work: a sensibility, a sense of order, always threatened to
emerge, but it hadn't yet, and I wasn't sure I cared to midwife it
even if I had been able, for then he would become a *writer,* then
he would produce *literature,* and I couldn't calculate how much
this might cost him. The first thing he ever handed in, the second
week of class, I read cold, aloud, dissembling my own shock as I
went, and three ladies of a certain age therewith dropped the
course. Which was surely just as well. Almost a year later, in
February of '66, I received a letter from Los Angeles, where he had
gone to seek his fortune. In moving from one coast to the other
he had lost all his manuscripts, and needing them now for one
reason or another he wondered if I had had the foresight and the
interest, given their obvious merit and high level of lubricity, to
have them Xeroxed while they were in my possession, in which case
he would be glad if I sent them along. He seemed fairly certain that

I'd had it done. An almost perfect arrogance. But he was right, he
was the dirtiest writer I have ever read. I wish I *had* reproduced
that endless copybook scrawl, I would certainly share it with you.
Reading him, that night, I was as embarrassed as I had been the
first time, this time for Christa's sake, slurring the "cocksuckers"
and the "cuntlappers" and the "prick testing the hairy asshole"
(male/male, this was), or less embarrassed than fearful, that
hearing me read the drivel she would associate me with it in her
mind, or not that either but fearful, yes, that exposing her to so
blatant an account and not shooting it down in the discussion which
followed (or even if I had) would tend to condone or make seem
respectable her own near-obsessional (if less graphic) concern with
sexuality. I followed up with Mrs. Hale, a drastic change of pace,
though I was not too much more comfortable reading the one than
the other. And finished with Mrs. Baldakian, a sweetfaced Jewish
woman in her forties married to an Armenian, whose fiction for a
long while turned (as it did that night) entirely on retardation,
the condition afflicting her youngest child. It did not seem the
most promising subject matter, yet she managed to infuse it with
some poignancy, though it was not easy to determine if that
quality stemmed more from our awareness of her closeness to the
subject than from the work itself. She was another of those who
puts a large trust in life—if I suggested that some incident or phrase
had not come off, taxed our sense of pace or credibility, she would
say, less carping than bewildered, "But Mr. Sams, it really *happened* that way," and I could never do more than rejoin lamely
that this wasn't always enough. Eventually I persuaded her to have
a go at something different, someone else's tragedy; a kind, cooperative lady, she produced a long story of abortion, desertion,
and cancer among Irish Catholics, possibly plucked from the One
Hundred Neediest Cases, not badly done, an improvement on her
earlier efforts, but by that time, mid-May, I was having trouble
maintaining real interest in the job.

So we got through the time. An average night. Eight cigarettes
smoked. Mrs. Hale waylaid me on some allegedly literary matter
before I could escape; I told Christa to wait for me in the lobby. I

waited a moment after Mrs. Hale left, assembled my papers, and took the elevator down. She was turning the leaves of the mobile bulletin board: concerts, tutors, dramatic productions, cars for sale, charter flights, shared auto rides to distant places.

"Sarkissian. Want to get a beer?"

"Do you?"

"You bet."

I took her arm, we walked into the evening.

"Your football player was very chatty on the way down."

"What about?"

"What I was doing there, who I was . . ."

(He tried to pick her up, that blundering Neanderthal?)

"Normal, healthy, young man's interest."

"Yes."

"What did you make of Delgado?"

"Which one was that?"

"The dirty one."

"Oh. Young, kind of feisty . . ."

"What's that mean?"

"Feisty? Like a little dog, snapping at your heels."

"That's a nice word. I've heard it, but I never knew what it meant. Well, this is it, the face of a great university. How does it stack up to Berkeley?"

She shrugged. "Less pretty. Much too citified."

"We had a tree once, but it died."

I waited, drymouthed, looking forward to the beer, hoping she would volunteer some comment on my overall performance, flattering or otherwise, but not terribly surprised when she did not. In the crowded, noisy bar, surrounded by the young, loosened by the first few slugs, I took over both our roles, deprecating the teaching post, or myself in it, then defending the action as a harmless holding of the line. The thing I had to do was finish *Gino Travels*, then wait; they would come flooding in, the offers and sinecures, Writer-in-Residence here, teach one course a week for fifteen thousand there, all over the vast, culture-hungry reaches of the nation, Arizona, Iowa, Colorado, places even closer to her home, and wouldn't that be nice? I wouldn't mind a year or so in the Bay Area, I told her, on a fat salary and with a sexy, native guide . . . and on along these lines, then the one beer too many (she still nursed her first), and we taxied home, already spending my future, but what the hell, I was not destitute now, and the basket was firmly on my head, I was pointed squarely toward the market.

7

The Voice Project:
An Idea for Innovation in
the Teaching of Writing*

JOHN HAWKES

For the past ten years, briefly at Harvard and then at Brown University, I have taught two kinds of writing courses, the advanced course intended for students interested specifically in fiction, and the intermediate writing course intended for students with only an ill-defined interest in improving their use of written prose. My commitment to this latter course has always been of a special kind, since it is here that the student's confrontation with language has been most pressing and that his personal growth has been most at stake. Though I have never thought of the intermediate writing course as "creative" in any exclusive sense, I have always approached the varied activity of this kind of course with a belief in creative attitudes and in the capacity of all students to be imaginative. The task has been to encourage the non-fiction writing student to discover himself as the center of a writing

* The Voice Project was hosted by Stanford University and supported under a grant from the U.S. Department of Health, Education and Welfare. Other writers in the project included William Alfred, Sylvia Berkman, Jerome Charyn, Mitchell Goodmann, Leo Litwak, Clive Miller, and Mark Mirsky. Copies of the "Voice Project" (ERIC accession Number ED 018 422) are available from ERIC document Reproduction Service, National Cash Register Company, 4936 Fairmont Avenue, Bethesda, Maryland 20014.

process which results in a personal or identifiable prose, rather than in "machine" or "voiceless" prose.

The operation of the class is simple. The students are required to write fifty pages during a semester; they are expected to participate in class discussions two hours a week and to make as much use of individual conferences with the instructor as possible; they are encouraged but not required to do related reading wherever possible; they are required to undertake short weekly writing exercises for the first half of the semester, after which they are given complete freedom to pursue the kinds of writing they are most interested in. At the outset the writing exercises are crucial and are concerned with problems of conception, method, and form, so that the area of subject matter is left entirely to the individual student. Typical exercises are to create the impression of imminent motion in a still object; to handle an event or idea in terms of past and present time; to handle an idea in terms of action and an action in terms of reflection; to handle any kind of material in the third person and then in the first person; to make the reader accept something extraordinary as commonplace and something commonplace as extraordinary. Aside from such exercises, the student is generally encouraged to write personal narrative during the first semester, though most students enrolling in the course came to personal narrative with surprise and an understandable resistance. But the point is that personal narrative forces the student to deal with memory, time, and himself as the center of the writing process and allows him to handle both concrete and abstract experience in a single piece of writing. In this way coherence becomes tangible and ideas emerge as dramatic entities. Underlying the course effort as a whole is the concept of voice—the one fictional concept which to me is most relevant to human growth and to communication in general. It is the concept that I have found most helpful as a teacher of so-called non-literary students, which is to say that it has been a means for helping students to change their writing while discovering that writing is a meaningful, rather than remote and mechanical, kind of behavior. To me, voice stands as one alternative to the sometimes crippling, external logic of formal rhetoric or the various other rationalistic approaches to writing which can never allow teacher and student to work together in one of our most difficult areas on the basis of a truly common understanding.

There are three ways of looking at the concept of voice. It is first of all the instrument of speech; in writing it may be taken to mean the summation of style; but also in writing it may be taken to mean the whole presence of the writer-as-writer rather than the writer-as-man. Writing is often more true to the self than is speaking, but at least writing should be as true to the self as is speaking.

Two quotations from the essay "Voice as Summons for Belief"* by Walter J. Ong, S.J., clarify and enlarge the implications of this subject:

> Speaking and hearing are not simple operations. Each exhibits a dialectical structure which mirrors the mysterious depths of man's psyche. As he composes his thoughts in words, a speaker or writer hears these words echoing within himself and thereby follows his own thought, as though he were another person. Conversely, a hearer or reader repeats within himself the words he hears and thereby understands them, as though he were himself two individuals. This double and interlocking dialect . . . provides the matrix for human communication. The speaker listens while the hearer speaks.

> Every human word implies not only the existence—at least in the imagination—of another to whom the word is uttered, but it also implies that the speaker has a kind of otherness within himself. He participates in the other to whom he speaks, and it is this underlying participation which makes communication possible. The human speaker can speak to the other precisely because he himself is not purely self, but is somehow also other. His own "I" is haunted by the shadow of a "thou" which it can never exorcise.

This thinking indicates that if we begin with "voice" as a concept particularly relevant to writing, we are taken ultimately—but in a special way—to the areas of psychology, literature, philosophy, and religious studies. The mere effort to write is filled with human resonance.

* From the book by Walter J. Ong, *The Barbarian Within* (Macmillan, 1962).

It is unlikely that the voice that emerges from writing will ever correspond exactly with the voice that emerges in speech. But even if these voices were equatable, it is extremely difficult to help the student to arrive at an actual comprehension of the writing voice as single, palpable, real. It is far easier to respond to the speaking voice, and yet within the limitations of an ordinary classroom even the speaking voice, as something with which to work concretely, is hardly available. In other words, until recently it had not occurred to me to attempt to work directly and diversely with the relationship between the "visceral" speaking voice of a person and his writing voice as it emerges from the page. But it now seems to me essential to explore fully this many-sided relationship.

In 1964 I spent several months working in close association with the Actor's Workshop in San Francisco, and it was this for me entirely new and intense involvement in theater life that convinced me that it was essential to approach the teaching of writing in terms of visible behavior as well as in terms of already written words. During rehearsals I was constantly moved by a single observation. That is, the progressive and externally evident effort of the actor working in the rehearsal area corresponded to a creative process which previously I had thought existed only as a psychological process within the individual man or artist. In other words, I was able to see something very like the writing process being acted out unintentionally by people who, as actors in a community situation, were nonetheless closely related to the "silent" writer. I became increasingly aware that acting, which reveals the almost immediately perceivable relationship between gesture and word, could be a very real means for bridging the various distances that exist in writing courses and for making concrete the problems and realities of voice.

One further personal experience crystallized the possibilities. I was able to visit an acting class taught by Gerald Hiken at Stanford University. Several problems were taken up during the hour, but one in particular was relevant to reading, behavior, discovery of the self, and expansion of personal capabilities and understanding— and hence relevant also to writing.

A young student stood before the group, folded his hands, raised his eyes toward the ceiling lights, and recited a Shakespeare lyric. The lyric was about summer as the season of love, and several times during his recitation the student was obliged to imitate the sounds of the cuckoo. The first reaction for the student spectators—to the effect that the recitation had been ironic—initiated a discussion of the lyric itself. Next the teacher asked another member of the class to sit in a chair on the stage with the first student and established this second student as someone who had heard bad news and needed not practical help but consolation. As soon as he heard this situation described, the second student wisely put his head in his hands. The reciter's task was to "give" the sufferer the lyric. The change in the spoken lyric was considerable. Next the teacher asked the first student to think of something personal and pleasurable—in this case a field recalled from childhood—and to recite the lyric. Lastly the teacher asked the first student to look directly at his audience, which he had not done until this moment, and to give the audience the lyric. Now the lyric emerged not as inappropriately ironic but as warm, light, and subtly and meaningfully humorous. In it was evident a definite life so that the sounds of a cuckoo, for instance, became a simple clear song instead of the vehicle for a young person's discomfort. In the discussion that followed, the teacher suggested that the physical limits of one student's voice in part accounted for the ironic stance he assumed no matter what role or piece of literature he confronted.

This kind of total and active involvement in literature seems to me essential, and suggests that we might well think of exploring the theater to make the learning experience a dramatic reality. At least theater techniques are particularly appropriate to all kinds of writing courses.

Background and Major Problems Under Consideration

The Voice Project emerged as an idea at a meeting of the Panel of Educational Research and Development in Washington in May,

1965. At the Tufts Seminar to Initiate New Experiments in Undergraduate Instruction, this idea was discussed and expanded by
members of the English Group until it assumed a crudely written
shape which became the basis for the formal proposal submitted to
the Office of Education. At two follow-up meetings for writers held
early in 1966 at Sarah Lawrence College and Columbia University,
the idea was reinforced while we accumulated further examples of
the kinds of teaching we wanted to try.

There was general agreement among the Tufts Seminar participants that nothing less than a revolution in present literary taste
and values as well as in our ideas about language is needed if
higher education is not to become increasingly remote from life
itself and increasingly meaningless to younger people. And further,
there was general agreement that we should in fact continue to try
to teach writing in college and that merely to abandon so-called
Freshman English would solve nothing (though we all considered
such words as "Freshman," "Freshman English," etc., to be deplorable); that writers—poets, fiction writers, playwrights, essayists
—should be involved in the teaching of writing; and finally, that it
made sense to focus on problems of writing in the first year of
college, but that we could not really begin to help the student make
writing an effective, pleasurable, and truly necessary part of his life
without the help of teachers from many fields and a total collaboration between teachers and students from elementary school to
graduate school.

The experiment was conducted within the context of the required
Freshman English course at Stanford University. At the outset, it
was agreed that the teaching in this experiment was intended to
fulfill the general objectives of Freshman English, which, as expressed by Albert Guerard, were "to develop the ability to write
effectively and the ability to read literature with discernment and
pleasure." On the other hand, the particular nature of the project
created special staffing and teaching problems and requirements.
Among these were (1) that the writer-teachers involved in the
project be recruited from a variety of colleges and universities as
well as from Stanford, (2) that each of these writer-teachers devote

full time to his class of twenty students, (3) that each writer-teacher carry out his work with the help of a graduate assistant with whom he would share all phases of the work and with whom he would attempt to achieve genuine colleagueship, (4) that the graduate assistants be drawn at least in part from areas other than English, and (5) that students participate in the project on a volunteer basis.

Shortly after the approval of our proposal by the Office of Education, we gathered a staff consisting of seven writer-teachers in addition to myself (and representing such diverse institutions of higher education as Harvard, Wellesley, San Francisco State, and The City College of the City University of New York), along with nine assistants who were doing graduate work in English, history, communications, education, and creative writing.

In the summer preceding this 1966–67 year a questionnaire was sent to the entire freshman class giving them a series of Freshman English options. Out of approximately 1,300 freshmen, 500 expressed interest in working in the Voice Project, and from these we selected 100 students to participate in the program. This selection was made at random except that we preserved the general Stanford ratio of three male students for each female student and selected students so that in each class of twenty, six geographical areas of the United States were represented.

As stated earlier, Voice Project classes were intended to involve the student as totally as possible in the act of writing; therefore, they depended on team teaching, on establishing total colleagueship between teachers and students, on sharing materials from class to class, and on helping the student to base his thinking and writing on as much activity as possible.

Throughout all of our activities we were attempting to make the word "voice" meaningful and useful for the student and were attempting to clarify the implications and possibilities for this term as a teaching method. We wanted the student to know that the sound of his voice conveys something of his personality; that this personal intonation might well relate to the diction and rhythms of his writing; that a professional writer has a kind of total presence that can be perceived and responded to as authorial "voice"; that there is a difference between "voice" and style; that reading aloud is a way to achieve dramatic comprehension of literature as well as a better understanding of what may be happening in a student's own writing. To us, then, "voice" meant (1) personality as heard in speech, (2) the kind of understanding we are able to "hear" in the voice of someone reading aloud, (3) the author's presence that we "hear" when we read silently, and (4) the various roles we sometimes assume in writing. Most of our classes were efforts to develop these ideas.

Our classes also encouraged the student to perceive the beauties of so-called everyday language, whether spoken or written, so that he could respond to such language as if it were, in fact, a literary text. And, conversely, our purpose in some classes was to help the student respond to significant literary works of art with the same intensity he was likely to bring to the language of his friends or to the language he generally heard around him. Often our efforts to develop the above specific notions or functions of "voice" were efforts to heighten perception; to make the student sensitive to other kinds of language; to help him to see behavior, physical gesture, and vocal gesture as forms of expression related to verbal language. The exercises we developed were intended to do all this.

Approximately one-third of Voice Project freshmen participated in experimental teaching projects in neighboring secondary and elementary schools. Generally, our students worked in teams of two or three students, were for the most part accompanied in their work by a writer-teacher or a graduate assistant, and spent from one to two hours a week in the classes with younger students. They worked with students ranging from pre-school disadvantaged students to second- and third-grade students to a somewhat mixed group of eighth-grade students with above-average abilities to a group of high school sophomores. Naturally, much of the activities in schools was similar to that in the Stanford classes. However, our efforts in the schools were at times more specifically aimed at clarifying and expressing ideas of voice for these younger students.

Particularly important to this experiment would be a summer teaching project involving intensive work with Negro students. The summer phase of the Voice Project was an integral part of the College Readiness Program at the College of San Mateo, which brought sixty-five Negro high school graduates from San Mateo County to the campus for course work, tutoring, and work-study jobs for a six-week period. As part of their preparation for entering the College of San Mateo in the fall, each of these students was required to take a special non-credit course in English. The Voice Project provided the equivalent of this course for thirty of the sixty-five students.

Our summer staff consisted of two Stanford graduate students and seven Stanford undergraduates who had been in the Voice Project at Stanford and had taught in the local schools throughout the year. The San Mateo students were divided into three groups, as was our staff. Each of the three Stanford teaching teams operated autonomously, the entire staff meeting formally twice a week to exchange ideas and discuss mutual problems. The undergraduates worked closely together so that there existed a constant dialogue about successful and unsuccessful teaching units and teaching techniques. Classes met for an hour and a half a day, five days a week.

The San Mateo students had been average students in remedial and non-academic high school courses. On the Nelson-Denny Reading Test they scored at the 8.5 grade level in overall reading skills. Their average reading speed was less than 180 words a minute. They had experienced so much failure in school and had been told so often that they should not take difficult courses that most of them had little or no self-confidence. Obviously the attitude of these students toward school was generally negative, and they resented being forced to attend what they thought would be dull, irrelevant courses taught by condescending white teachers.

Our objectives for the summer (to help the student discover the excitement of spoken and written language, etc.) were similar to those we attempted to carry out at Stanford. But in the summer program it was especially important that we find ways to help build the student's confidence in himself by working with his own language and demonstrating what he himself could do with it, to remove fear and punishment from the task of writing, and to eliminate negative attitudes toward teachers by participating with the students in each assignment and in-class exercise.

Conclusions and Recommendations

Even though this first year was devoted to exploration rather than to precise evaluation, it is still clear that we were more successful in achieving some objectives than others. In general, "voice" did in fact serve as a "focus of multiform innovation." Throughout this year we stimulated interest in writing on the Stanford campus and in the local schools and involved many different kinds of teachers and students in our efforts. The teaching of writing demands just this kind of total collaboration—between writers, teachers, college students and school students, teachers in other colleges and universities and professional schools, and members of the community interested in writing.

In teaching experimental classes, we were not able to provide materials and circumstances which involved large numbers of students in the creation of games and compositions based on recorded sounds and visual materials, nor did we explore dramatic techniques as fully as we might have. Only one of our writer-teachers was also a dramatic director, and his presence was simply not enough to generate extensive experimenting with forms of behavior which are, in effect, analogous to verbal expression. This general inability to develop forms of expression analogous to writing was a special problem at elementary and pre-school levels, where we probably did not contribute as much to the lives of younger students as we learned from them. Further, we had intended giving these younger students anthologies of their spoken compositions, but the pressures of the year precluded this possibility. These ideas deserve more work in the future.

Then, too, our efforts to help our Stanford students to function at least in part as teachers in the schools were sometimes less effective than they might have been, due to the necessary flexibility and spontaneity of the first year. That is, some of the less structured teaching moments were difficult for the students.

Throughout the year we attempted to introduce popular materials into our classes and, as indicated in the summaries of experimental classes, tried to help our students to read with greater precision and dramatic involvement. At best we were partially successful in these efforts. We feel that future programs should concentrate especially on exploring popular culture as a subject worthy of intensive and imaginative study.

It goes without saying that the most important aspect of this project was the use of the concept of voice and the use of recording devices to help students at different educational levels and of different social backgrounds to write more effectively. Involved in this specific effort were various aims which deserve comment:

To compare qualities of personality revealed in a person's speech with corresponding qualities evident in his writing. Our work in early Stanford classes and in the San Mateo project at the end of the year supported the idea that these correspondences exist and can be most important in helping the student to recognize himself in his writing. Toward the end of the year, while working individually with Stanford students, it appeared that a student could profitably revise his work not only by listening to repeated readings of passages of his own prose revealing desirable rhythms, but also by imitating the actual intonations evident in the recordings of his own voice.

To enable students to read aloud repeatedly and listen back to their writing in order to discover such things as changes in voice, evasiveness, etc. Many of our group discussions, especially small-group discussions, involved this kind of activity, which, in general, was most successful. Repeated listenings and the reactions of other students enabled a young writer to hear and perceive intellectually those moments when his lack of understanding or emotional con-

fusion (excessive emotional involvement) caused him to shift dis-
quietingly into different voices or into various kinds of voiceless or
machine prose.

*To enable the student to "talk out" certain materials he has writ-
ten about in order to discover new materials and new attitudes.*
Despite the considerable time we devoted to work with individual
students, we were not able to spend as much time as we should
have in this kind of time-consuming activity. When we were able to
work alone with the student, who would read aloud an inadequate
passage and recall or discuss on tape experiences or ideas dealt
with in the passage, we invariably found that the student gained
new awareness of vital materials and attitudes that he had overlooked or suppressed in his writing. In these cases the truth or
accuracy or concreteness of what was achieved in speech (and had
been heard on tape) in a sense compensated for the deficiencies
of the student's writing and served as a basis for revision. This sort
of session was not intended to be therapeutic or psychological. New
materials and actual tones of voice exposed in these sessions inevitably prompted discussion of language itself. We should make
much greater efforts to work along these lines.

*To encourage students to record the speech of other people
which they may then study.* This kind of literal involvement with
the language of others was limited to perhaps half of our students,
but for these students the actual collecting of speech was a most
important learning experience. The discovery of living tellers of
folktales and discovery of how language functions in this particular
form; the collecting and study of individual stories and group dia-
logues of children which revealed subtleties, complexities, and
beauties of language comparable to those in certain books or
stories—all this was for our students actual, challenging, engaging.
One student went so far as to document the life and personality of
a friend by collecting tapes of her speech in a variety of situations
which she then compared to her formal written compositions, examination papers, and personal letters. We should find ways of
allowing many more students to become this actively concerned
with the language that exists around them.

To study the similarities and differences between the qualities of the speaker's voice audible in a tape recording and the qualities apparent in a transcript of the recording. In reading, writing about, and discussing tapes and transcripts of speakers outside the Stanford community, many of the participating Stanford freshmen learned to recognize certain formulas of speech and borrowed phrasing and worked with the loss which almost always took place between tape and transcript. On the other hand, these students also learned to recognize original rhythmical moments in transcripts which, in fact, began to suggest the speaker's audible voice. As suggested by many of the previous summaries of experimental sessions, much of our work was based on this activity and was at times extremely successful. We sometimes worked with individual students or with small groups of students on the problem of revision. If a student "talked out" his ideas and materials, he profited not only by uncovering new materials or new ideas but also by coming to perceive what were often extreme differences between the actual intonations of his voice and the transcribed language. He perceived the inadequacy of the language itself; he could attempt with some measure of success to find ways to incorporate into his writing certain qualities analogous to his spoken intonations. However, we were not able to do nearly enough of this kind of work. Future experimentation should concentrate on this activity.

To involve the student in group discussions and group story-telling sessions so that he may listen to his speech and study it in relationship to the speech of the other participants in the group. In several school classes this use of the tape recorder was clearly effective in helping students to learn about form and about the functions of language as well as to learn about themselves and their own uses of language. In addition, several Stanford classes found it profitable simply to replay, after a reasonable time lag, portions of particularly valuable class discussions, which the students could then respond to with critical detachment. Especially in light of the study of small-group behavior, this kind of effort deserves further exploration.

To enable the student to hear varying interpretations of his own writing. Obviously, we consider it important that the student hear his writing read aloud by those other than himself—other teachers, other students, writers and actors from the university or local community.

For the writers and teachers participating in this project the year's work at Stanford substantiates the value of some of our initial broad assumptions: that students should be encouraged to teach or tutor as part of their college experience; that writing should in fact be taught in college and should involve writers, teachers of widely differing experience, or simply anyone interested in teaching writing; and finally, that to teach writing by working with the relationship between speech and writing has significant possibilities of developing the verbal abilities of students at all educational levels. But for us the year's work was an exhaustive start which now suggests more clearly the considerable amount of work to be done in the future.

Despite this present year of Voice Project work, and all that we know about rhetoric as well as new developments in linguistics, it seems safe to say that there will never be any one way to teach writing and, further, that we really do not know very much about this process. Further work should probably be viewed first in terms of consortia of people and institutions or special centers or organizations within institutions.

In subsequent programs similar to this one, evaluative studies should be conducted within the classes; ideas and exercises should be further refined with particular emphasis on the use of materials at different age levels and with students of different language backgrounds. Future projects should include on their staffs not only writer-teachers but also psychologists whose interest in language, group behavior, and learning processes should help to define concepts of voice more specifically. Throughout this year we have in fact used such concepts actively and effectively, and yet we have not documented psychologically the existence of what we call the "writing voice." Both for the sake of teaching reading as well as writing, we should probably devise a series of psychological exercises based, for instance, on different examples of a writer's prose, in order to substantiate still more concretely the concept of voice. But specific research should be conducted, at least in part, by writers and psychologists together, on such subjects as gesture in speech, personality in speech, and prose rhythm. We do not want our students to write as they speak, but there are fundamental relationships between speech and writing which can be used to teach writing. All this is to say that a great deal of energy must yet be spent if we are to be able to teach what Robert Frost called "the sound of sense."

The Classroom Experience: Some Examples

By John Hawkes and Zeese Papanikolas—log by Zeese Papanikolas

October 19

Small-group meeting. We had asked students to write more about childhood. The assignment was in two parts—first, to write at most two pages creating an impression of something concrete or of a place or experience from childhood, and, second, to write at most two more pages handling these same materials analytically. Today's class was based on Jim Wright's impression/analysis about sitting on the chimney of his house as a boy. One question Jack and I decided in advance to take up was how to know the sex of this speaker. So we started by asking Paul, George, and Elaine to go into separate rooms and write imaginary pieces pretending to be children on the tops of chimneys. We were counting on Elaine to write unmistakably like a girl. While they were out of the room, the class heard Jim read his paper:

> Probably the most important part of our house was the roof, especially the red brick chimney near the north end. Many afternoons I would sit on top of this chimney and look at the scenery. To the north were two reservoirs nestled between rolling farmland. Occasionally as I watched, red balers would cut through the blue-grass dropping heavy bales where the grass had been.
> On the west and south were more frame houses not so different from ours. But this wasn't the town; the houses weren't packed

together. Each home had a large green yard filled with trees. Yet there weren't many houses and the rolling fields soon replaced them.

Toward the east lay the town (if you can call two thousand people a town). The business district was almost half a mile away at the bottom of the hill I was standing on and even it was hidden by trees. Beyond the town there were more houses climbing the gentle slopes toward farmland.

Somehow all of this was my little world, but even I didn't know why this view fascinated me. I didn't realize the beauty in the landscape, yet I often stood on the chimney and watched my world. For this reason the roof was the most important part of our house.

—Jim Wright

Jack's marginal comments:

"I would sit on top of this chimney"—lovely idea! but doesn't it need some sort of comment? After all, the experience is fairly unusual. Also, you might well convey (visualize) distance?

"Nestled," "gentle slopes," "fascinated"—who's speaking now?

The repetition in this last sentence is simply a kind of false ending—

Nice effort. This passage is fairly close to the natural rhythms and tones of your speaking voice, and does generate a pleasing quality out of "simple" prose. But I think you'll hear that many of these sentences are the same length and begin in the same way—perhaps because of a curious kind of restraint. Don't you hear considerable embarrassment in "this was my little world"?

Jim's reading was recorded on tape. We then taped Paul and George reading this same passage and compared the three versions of the piece. Jim's own reading was flat and did suggest a "country boy's" voice, which seemed appropriate to his world. Paul and George read quickly and (as someone said) as if they had never seen rolling country. Finally Elaine came in and read her imagined account:

(Oh, wow! It would sure be a long way to fall.)
There are three of Ting's balls that ended up on the roof when

I forgot to let go soon enough. And there's Dan's super ball that didn't quite make it over the roof like it was supposed to. (I always wondered what happened to it.)

I feel like if I stood up and started dancing, Mary Poppins would come out of the sky and play with me. It's jolly to be up so high and so far away from the rest of the people. It feels somehow very special.

Oh there goes Wendy Heffner playing her trumpet again. She's honestly improved quite a bit from a few months ago. You should have heard her then.

I really do feel like dancing or singing or something. When you sit on a chimney, you just can't sit there doing nothing. I guess looking at everything down below is fun enough, but somehow you can't look at it in the same way you do when you're down there yourself.

I honestly think that if I jumped off the chimney right now, I could fly. Or at least be able to walk around without falling down into our rose garden. (Ouch!) Maybe I'd better not try it. I could be wrong.

But I don't think so. . . .

—Elaine Smith

This was an exciting session and I think a great deal was accomplished. The students were able to hear the relaxed, slow, rather soft voice Jim used to read his piece, which helped them to talk about this writing on a quite technical level: short sentences, repetitive constructions, equal sentence length, a panoramic vision. Elaine's lively, childlike fantasy brought us to a discussion of "male" and "female" styles—immediacy and personal involvement of her interior monologue, compared to detached, ordered view in Jim's. Class ended, but most students stayed on and we discussed the second half of Jim's paper, a rather labored conceit comparing a storm to a battle:

Up here on our roof I can see everything a lot better. That's why I often come up to watch a storm march in. Far away I can see the battle raging. The silent cannons flash their warnings for the rest of the people to go to bed. I'm the only one left to watch as the storm marches on. A shell explodes softly in the distance. Then another. The explosions are much closer now. The air tingles with the fresh clean fumes of battle. As the storm gets closer the

racing breeze begins to roar in my ears. It surges into my lungs and
carries out the dust of everyday life. Bombs burst all around me;
the cannons and flare hurt my eyes. The mind thunders its message
—power, power, power.

Alone I wait to love the fury, to hear the living breath. It lifts me
from my earthly perch. Deep within the heart I'll hear the voice of
life. But the rains realize the danger and drive me from the heart
back to the roof-top perch. Back to a dry bed where the rest of the
people lay.

Jack's marginal comments:

My own feeling is that the storm is a good idea, but that the
contrast between adult metaphor and childish phrasing and short
sentences is unfortunately extreme. Paradoxically, if the metaphor
had been even more exaggerated it might have worked? The
second paragraph suggests a very different—and totally adult—
speaker, and part of this shift is due to prose rhythms becoming
metrical. Read the passage aloud. . . . Why are "rains realize" and
"rest of the people lay" a return to the child's voice?

Students discussed the idea that a change in visual perspective
might change the viewer's feelings about the scene, and were able
to see that the methodical slow detached voice of Jim's analysis
(summary of town, hay balers, etc.) wasn't appropriate to a dramatic scene, and (having "heard" his voice in that piece) to point
out shifts from adult to child stances, and the rather overblown
rhetoric in the second. We worried about the problem of a writer
attempting to assume a child's consciousness. George said that Jim's
reading of "power, power, power," did not convey any energy at all.
But the class liked Jim's own discovery of metaphor as a way to
create an impression of an experience and, despite all the problems
of "mixed" voices, thought he had handled the exercise well. We
briefly heard portions of George's piece and of Paul's. Not much
done with them, except to talk about falseness of a rhetorical cliché
in Paul's.

February 8

Meeting with nine. The plan was to work with "Hey, Bruce
Hopkins," a poem by a girl in Leo's (Leo Litwak's) section, about

a high school classmate who was a social outcast, was blind in one
eye, and who finally stabbed to death a girl working for his family.
(Jack had taken John Barth to Leo's class discussion of this poem
and both he and Barth, along with Mark Mirsky and Clive Miller,
had taped interpretive readings of the poem.)

> Hey, Bruce Hopkins, where are you going?
> With your glass eye
> And your dagger in your hand.
>
> Bruce Hopkins, are you tired
> Of life and men and women?
> Are you frightened of the empty socket your world has become?
> Do you scan the blurred horizon for a voice, an answer?
> A reason for your senseless loneliness?
> Bruce Hopkins, in the silent, ugly morning of tomorrow
> You wander—drunk, sinking, and submerged
> Quicksand smucking all around you
> Drawing you into a slimy trench
> Of confused hatred.
>
> Bruce Hopkins, can I reach you, can I help?
> Don't kill *me*—I feel for you Bruce,
> With your kitchen knife in one hand
> And your rotten eye. . . .
>
> And now, Bruce Hopkins, lying whitely in that bed,
> Chained, dazed.
>
> Why?
> Why?
>
> why not
>
>   —Helen Williams

We passed out the poem, Jack read it aloud in a monotone (what
he calls his "voiceless" reading), we again focused on the speaker,
and telling the students only that the poem was written by someone
in another class, asked the group to "type" the person addressing
Bruce Hopkins. Jim Kilgore thought that Bruce H. was himself the
speaker. Paul Raymore: someone who's alone, desirable, wants to

help—the ideal of womanhood. Jim Wright: a "do-gooder." Kathy Arbuckle: girl without anyone. Francie: a social worker, an "angel," certain amount of detachment and insincerity. Helene: girlfriend of alcoholic or dope addict. David Lam: older sister, mother. We exploited the "insincerity" motif in Francie's idea and found another word for it: detachment. Helene liked the poem but heard humorous elements in it: the first lines, beginning of the third stanza, the answer to the last question. She heard a popular song in the first line: "Hey Joe, where are you going with that gun in your hand." And Francie mentioned several other songs with this same formula. But the class kept resisting the idea of considering any action behind the poem: Francie going so far as to say that "Don't kill me" was metaphoric: "Don't kill my hope," or something of that nature. So to try to move from speaker to action we decided that each of us would "make up a story about the speaker in the poem":

> She walked up the stairs, down to the end of the hall, and slowly opened the bolted door directly facing her. Once inside the door, she was drawn to the French windows covering one side of the room. She looked out and down at the great expanse of green lawn below her.
> After a while she turned to face the now unbolted door, and, standing in the center of the room, her eyes followed the dark red wall paper and soon fell upon an old chest of drawers. Her gaze examined the chest and wondered as to what it held, but she didn't open one of its drawers for fear she would have guessed correctly.
> —Kathy Arbuckle

> Green grass glistened under a moist blanket of sparkling morning dew, and a lonely figure stepped out of the east. It was a girl; a girl with long, straight black hair that hung down her back and shimmered in the fresh sunlight with a life of its own. Her face was plain with a small petite nose, slightly upturned, and large, moist lips. . . .
> On the grass, huddled in a small brown bundle, was a puppy. A puppy with large doleful eyes and a small black nose, cold and wet. The girl approached and as she neared the puppy it gave a squeak of recognition. The girl's face softened and her deliberate graceful walk turned into a joyful dash to where the puppy lay,

cold and alone, in the grass. She took it up into her arms and it seemed at that moment, with the morning's newly risen sun as a background, that she was the picture of all things that go into womanhood: understanding, courage, tenderness, and deep feeling for life.

—Paul Raymore

She carried her lunch in a paper bag, wore a simple thin ribbon in her hair, walked always near the wall in crowded corridors, and shared a locker with a girl who stuck chewing gum on the inside of the locker door. And day after day she heard the banging of the third locker door away from hers, was aware of that boy who smashed steel against steel when the corridor was filled with noise and the smell of perspiration, was aware of the crashing sound and, within sight of that rough shoulder, was helpless, knowing all the while that she was a kind of victim who would feel his fingers on her arm or hear him speak. One night she dreamt of him and the next day, when everyone was laughing in the corridor, he was gone and there was nothing she could do but write a poem on the fly leaf of her ancient history text book.

—Jack Hawkes

At first everyone felt that Kathy's piece had very little to do with the poem, but we argued for her evocation of loneliness as starkly real, shocking, mysterious, talked about contrasting detail that creates isolation here, the "bolted door" that suggests the door to your own past as well as confinement, some powerful guilt. We worried considerably about Paul's piece—its sentimentality, the incongruity between the idealized girl and the unreal and senti-mentalized puppy. Here there were moments of embarrassed si-lence, maybe some indication that the students knew these materials and themes are important to Paul. Jack's piece brought us to the realization that the speaker in the poem was in some way Helen Williams herself and Chuck saw the loneliness of Jack's version of Helen Williams—"walking along the sides of the crowded halls," a "thin ribbon in her hair"; but Chuck asked, "If she's totally alone, how can she help as she claims in the poem?" And George an-swered: "That's the reason."

Jack tried to help the group into this idea of aloneness and help-

lessness as a possible strength and summarized the actions in the
pieces we'd heard (to enter a forbidden room; to cuddle a dog; to
walk alone in a crowded school and to dream and to write a poem).
He then shifted the discussion to the problem of Bruce's action,
asking what Bruce Hopkins had actually done—but the group
tended to resist the idea that he'd really done anything, so Jack
concentrated on the difference between "dagger" (the speaker's
naive poeticizing) and "kitchen knife," which was concrete, exact,
and could (in someone's words) be a thing of violence.

Here we listened to the taped readings of the poem by John
Barth and Clive. I worked hard on the possibilities of "Don't kill
me" as metaphoric, humorous, insincere—and finally Francie admitted that the cry might quite literally refer to a physical death
and be addressed to a killer—a possibility she didn't like to think
about. (Back to the "kitchen knife." We decided that Clive's "New
York taxicab driver" reading was exciting, funny, terrifying, but was
also imposed on the poem and might have been the result of his
own embarrassment. Barth's exaggerated reading of "Don't kill *me*
—I feel for you Bruce. . . ." confirmed the embarrassment idea:
something terrible had happened and the speaker (or poet) was
uncertain about her feelings or how to handle them.

One last reading by the poetess herself. We listed the characteristics of her voice and began getting nearer to the realities of the
poem by hearing the seriousness of her reading. She "cares," "loves
him," is "experienced—" "whispers," is "listless." Jack compared the
voice to that of a person in shock. He heard "tears and grief" in
the voice. Then he told the class about the circumstance behind
the poem and talked about the adolescent desire to "help," and the
suppression of the knowledge of what that help implied, and guilt
for not having given it. A naively sincere poem he called this. I
talked about the mixture of voices here as a reflection of the writer's
confused feelings—the warmth, detachment, and inadvertent humor
creating incompatible voices or possibilities.

Generally I was pleased that the students are managing to conceive of a speaker in such concrete and sometimes strangely accurate terms.

The Black Voice: Teaching at the College of San Mateo

By Thomas Grissom

I'm far from it, 'cause I've known days when there was no food in the house, and I was starving, and I didn't have anything to wear to school. I know what it's like to be hungry, dear boy.
—Frances Earle, July 26, 1967
(Student in Summer Readiness
Program, College of San Mateo)

"What's the tape recorder for?"
Gwen was the first in our class of eleven black students to speak. Kim and Mark—two Stanford freshmen who had been in the Voice Project classes of John Hawkes and Mark Mirsky, respectively— and I groped through the use of tapes. We hoped that they would warm to the novelty of a tape recorded on that first day and use it for telling a chain story. We could then play it back for them and convert the tape into a transcript so that it could be read.

But we were taken aback when they unanimously agreed that they wrote better than they spoke. The opposite was true for most of the white students I had taught. I now believe they were really saying, "As a teacher, you will probably prefer my writing to my speaking." They were unconsciously emphasizing the disparities between their habits of speech, which are "taught out" by our society's schools, and their style of writing, which is a reflection of the mainstream American usage. The students had been made to feel guilty about the way they spoke.

"Well, man, I really need your English class."
Lee Cohens, an outspoken affable boy of eighteen who worked nights as a janitor at the Ampex plant, had just read a three-page transcript of the story he had told the class on the first day. The story was about an imaginary trip he had taken to Rome during the weekend following his graduation from high school. His telling of the tale had dominated our entire class, but after reading what he had said, he was disappointed and ashamed.

He couldn't tell me why he felt that way. The other kids helped him out. "It's not 'proper.'" "There are too many mistakes in there." Lee finally burst out, "This is pool hall talk." Of course it was. The language was imprecise and full of Negro jargon. It was more oral than written and appeared flat and dull when there wasn't instant human feedback or physical contact for the non-verbal aspects of communication. But it *sounded* beautiful! There were rhythms and inflections in that speech that I had never heard before.

We wanted to prove this to Lee. The night before this class we had prepared a tape of a white student from Stanford reading Lee's transcript without ever hearing him tell the story.

After discussing the story during the class we turned the recorder on, and Lee heard the white girl trying to tell his story. He was amazed to hear her imitation of the Negro dialect and accent. Near the end of the transcript there are the two sentences: "Seem like they celebrate *anything*. Yeah, but I was really happy from celebratin', celebrating graduation, you know, but they was doin' it." The girl read the underlined words the same way she had always read underlined words on a printed page. She gave them emphasis by reading louder.

After pointing this out to Lee we turned his tape on and listened to these original passages. He hadn't raised his voice at all. His voice had dropped in intensity. It was emphasis in his way. With a typewriter, the secretary could only underline it, and with a printed page, the student could only raise her voice.

I also showed him where he had said, "It was real nice, and you know they was more like relatives to strangers, you know, you'd walk past them and they'd have somethin' to say, you know, they— you'd smile and that was *it*. Yeah, it was real nice." We listened to him saying it over the tape recorder. His voice was marvelous, full of warmth and tenderness. On the transcript, however, the sentences appeared plain and confused. He was trying to say that these people treated him like a relative. They treated strangers as if they were relatives. His spoken voice conveyed this feeling, this impression. But when put to paper it was lost. I think this moment marked the start of a change in attitude by these black students toward their speech. Perhaps I should have urged the transformation of these spoken strengths into their writing, but I felt it was more important for the students to see the value in something they already possessed—their own speaking voices.

"Don't get all excited about the way I talk 'cause I know where it leads to. I want some of the stuff you're puttin' down."

A week later Lee confronted me with a problem that all of us from Stanford had been ignoring or afraid to consider. Through our sincere enthusiasm for their class participation and early writing, some of the black students thought we were romanticizing their spontaneity of thought and speech. This is how a well-intentioned white teacher patronizes a black student. "Just be yourself when you write." "If you come to class, you'll get no lower than a C." "It's more important what you say, than how you say it." They had been told this before and the result had been poor grades, remedial courses, crippled reading skills, and a detached, breezy attitude toward writing.

Lee wanted "what I was puttin' down" because it would lead to that "fat check, baby." His motives were clear and precise. He felt no need to hide them behind some doubletalk about the joy of learning. And he wanted to make sure I knew all of this. "Don't tell me grammar and spelling ain't important. That's how you get a job."

I admired his honesty although it was upsetting for us from Stanford. He was telling too much of the truth about all of us. Our first reaction was to do what Lee wanted us to do—a much easier teaching task. We could eliminate the mechanical errors in the class's writing and take satisfaction in the belief that their writing had, indeed, improved. This illusion was shattered within a few days, shortly after we had spent an entire class "correcting" sentences.

"Tom, you really got to me! You said, 'Hell! Who would write somethin' like this!'—and I wrote it! I was mad at you that day—I coulda cut your neck off."

Bonnie and I were disappointed in each other. She had turned in a nice, clean, relatively flawless piece of garbage and I was angry at her dishonesty. She had written the "proper" way, the grammatical way, and had all the opinions that she thought a teacher would expect to find within the "right kind" of writing:

> To me the 4th of July is suppose to be a day that all Americans give thanks for their independence. Because on this Great Day the Declaration of Independence was signed making all Americans independent. This day should be a day of flag flying. Or a big parade with people standing on the side line cheering and waving flags, showing that they really appreciate this great day. . . .
>
> —Bonnie

In my anger, I was revolting against the very practice I had been encouraging. Bonnie and the class had proved to me and themselves that preoccupation with grammar and spelling would only lead to improved grammar and spelling. And the emphasis on these problems led them away from honesty, sincerity, and feeling. It encouraged students to make a number of assumptions about their teachers' expectations, the "right" way to write, separation of the classroom from the experiences of life, and the necessity of keeping certain "things" out of your writing.

The class had been asked to write about the Fourth of July. The papers were, in fact, relatively free of usage of errors, but the content was characterized by lifeless language and stereotyped opinion. They read like small-town Kansas newspapers and elementary school civics textbooks. The expression of beliefs, which we knew were not their own, with words taken from English-class spelling lists and placed in sentences which could be diagrammed for structure with three parallel lines, was more than we could take:

> I feel that the Fourth of July is a day when everyone can have fun and express their feelings.
>
> —Cubie

> The Fourth of July is a day when each person in the U.S. relaxes, goes on a picnic, watches fireworks, or visits friends.
>
> —Lynne

Though we could have spent a great deal of time criticizing these papers, we chose to emphasize what was most obvious to us all. The passion of their beliefs and the excitement of their language which we had come to know in class were absent in this writing. That we could recognize this was not only a criticism of their writing but a revelation about themselves—they had distinctive voices that people could hear. And, lastly, we could share the blame because we had emphasized form and structure to them before and while they were writing.

A few hours after class I reminded Lee of his earlier statement about grammar and spelling. He replied, "I wanna get that job, but not so bad that I wanna lose my voice."

"Now you go back to the middle of that thing you wrote and you'll see you sound like you're tryin' to be cool. But in the end it sound completely serious."

Skip wrote only a few times during the summer. But he was the best teacher in the class. He was a careful listener and observer, who put his abilities to work criticizing the other students' written work. He used his knowledge of the class and his sensitive ears to identify anonymous student writers and to differentiate between writing done by girls and boys.

Skip was verbal, and he was in a class which demanded that he tell stories, make up accents and rhythms, imitate the sounds of old age and youth, and identify and criticize written passages imitating speech. More than any other student, he grasped the focus of each class meeting and would guide the discussion with his own questioning and critical remarks.

Skip never let anyone know much about himself. It was easier for him to act, imitate, and criticize than to reveal. As we moved through the summer, however, this detachment began to fade. The kids would challenge him on his ideas about writing and his personal beliefs. "I just don't talk that way, Skip." "I wasn't brought up to believe that." "You never write anything, Skip, who are you to say?" He had to reply and defend himself. He had to be *a* teacher instead of *the* teacher.

Slowly, a new Skip emerged, on paper and on tape. "The forth of July is for the wight man." "I believe it's a dog eat dog world."

"My daddy never taught me nothin'. I learned how to play basketball and baseball myself with a lotta time and embarrassment." He was the only student who always used the word "black" instead of "Negro."

A person left closed up and tight by a society and its schools, a boy whose obvious abilities had been crippled and blunted—though he never totally accepted us, the Voice Project was a release for what was his and may be most important to his life: his knowledge about sounds and language left to him by a society which forced him to listen more often than speak. He drew upon what he knew about speech to criticize other students' writing and to dramatize other authors' characters. As he heard tapes of himself and read transcripts of his remarks, he was no longer ashamed. During the last week, when he read the students' writing on the Detroit and Newark riots, he was impressed by what they had done. And his last in-class remarks gave some hint as to when and why Skip will begin to write.

Discussing Eric's paper on the riots:

SKIP: I didn't imagine nobody in this class would write like that.

GWEN: Eric usually didn't like to write.

SKIP: This was on a subject he wanted to write about.

ERIC: I'll write when I have somethin' to write.

SKIP: Tell 'em, brother. A whole different way of lookin' at things.

ERIC: When you read what Johnson say— Well, I disagree with 'im so I just start to writin'.

SKIP: You sits up and writes and can't stop.

ERIC: And then it just kept comin', I just kept writin'.

"That writing's so bad Valerie's done asleep."

That was Gwen's way of criticizing the following passage:

> The upsurge probably reflects as well the realization of increasing number of the world's youth that world peace probably can be accomplished twenty years faster by a deliberate design-science revolution than by waiting for the inadvertent twenty-years-later-fallout into the standard-of-living-advancing-commerce

of the accelerating ephemeralization, as originally promulgated by only a wide variety of basic fear motivations, all of which result in the self-protective world-munitions racing. The world youth intuit that the twenty-year difference could be the difference between humanity's success or extinction.

We had chosen a passage from Buckminster Fuller's personal essay in the reunion book for his graduating class at Harvard College to demonstrate the importance of authorial purpose and reading audience in certain kinds of writing. Together we staggered through a reading and then patiently defined all the words which the class didn't know. After reading the passage once again, the class began to understand what was being said. Skip suggested rather blandly, "This man is against the draft."

But Gwen saw even more. Half the class was asleep or studying psychology. "Why is everybody so bored, Gwen?" "Because this man writes to put to asleep." She had seen the negative effect of writing which is meaningless to specific audiences.

We woke everyone up and in a few minutes had them all eagerly discussing the importance of considering the writer's purpose and his audience, how scientists and "people who go to Harvard" talk and write, and how choice of words can affect the ease of reading and understanding. If language could put certain people to sleep, it could also be used to attract their attention, persuade them, and change their opinions.

"It could be a girl saying that or a boy. So I'm not voting."

Jackie didn't say a word until the fourth day of our class. He wouldn't come the first day. The second day he slouched in a chair where he hid behind a pair of blue sunglasses and listened. The third day he faked reading a book for psychology. On the fourth day he wouldn't sit at the table. He sat in a chair along the wall, still wearing the "shades," but following the class discussion.

The students had done in-class writing on the two previous days but Jackie had refused to write. Now they were discussing a dittoed sheet on which each student's writing appeared, anonymously, and in parallel columns for each day. On both days they had been asked to react and respond to two different tapes of sounds of war, rainfall, truck sirens, and pedestrians. Tuesday's papers had been dull listings of the various sounds with a few attempts to tie the sounds together in a story. The first writing we received from the class—it was monotonous, dry, unimaginative, and barely readable.

On Wednesday, without returning any papers, we talked about the words "reaction," "response," and "imagination." We differentiated between descriptions which merely identify and descriptions which are the controlled release of imagination in response to a stimulus. Wednesday's writing was so startlingly different that we decided to contrast the two assignments for each student on the same dittoed page.

<table>
<tr><td align="center">TUESDAY</td><td align="center">WEDNESDAY</td></tr>
<tr><td>The noises that I've heard seem to pertain to the military; all the strange noises had to do with the military, the target practice, and I guess that rumbling noise were tanks, and also the men doing exercises and the siren maybe that was an alert signal for the men to go into action, for instance we have practice fire drills, maybe that siren was for them to practice, in case of an attack.</td><td>It reminds me of rain falling on cement when I have to go out in the cold to get the Sunday paper or when I'm stuck on the sidewalk and there isn't anyone around, waiting for my dad whose about 10 minutes late—It reminds me of San Francisco—all the fog and the noise of traffic busily buzzing along —and it also reminds me of a day at CSM.</td></tr>
</table>

(Both pieces of writing are by the same student on successive days.)

After a short discussion about which papers they preferred and why, we asked if they could decide upon the sex of the writer whose work appeared on the list. Jackie's sunglasses came down off his nose. He looked at me for the first time. The students had begun to argue among themselves. "What do you mean, 'no woman would say that'?" "Well, it sounds like a boy here (Wednesday) but not in this one (Tuesday)." After fifteen minutes on the first two papers we took a vote on the writer's sex. Jackie refused to vote. The vote was 5 to 4 and the majority was right. It was a girl.

We went on to the next two samples. Jackie put his sunglasses in his pocket, stood up, and swaggered down to a vacant chair at the end of the table. He smiled with feigned confidence and remained silent. The second discussion was even more furious. The class began to concentrate on the second day's writing more and more to determine the author's sex. "You can't tell nothin' from the first column." "There's people in the last writing." The vote was 6 to 3 for a girl. This time the majority was wrong. Jackie still didn't vote.

Now Jackie began to look at the dittoed page. "Who wrote #3?" Again the discussion focused on the second column.

At first it reminded me of the War in Vietnam. A sergeant in the background giving orders to his men to fire. I mean the sound of guns firing made me think of the war . . . People riding around in the Africa jungle and I could hear elephants in the background. Maybe on a safari in jeeps . . . A soldier giving orders to other soldiers about handling rifles and marches back and forth. I could hear the stamping of feet very loudly. . . . A buzzer was ringing very loudly. It sounded like a warning or something.

I'm sitting in my front room, looking out at the cars going along in the rain. People are walking to and fro trying to get home and out of the rain. My house is near an airport and I can hear a plane coming in for a landing. I imagine the runway lights must be blaring along the runway. I have a warm sense of security, me and my house and the rain outside. The rain can't get in, and I don't want to go out. The passengers are leaving the plane to go home. Relatives are waiting happily to see them.

They began to point out that because on Wednesday we had urged personal and imaginative responses, it was easier to detect the writer behind these descriptions than the rigid descriptions that were written on Tuesday. Finally, Jackie spoke. In the end he did vote—on the winning side of a 7 to 3 decision that it was a girl writing.

"I felt very inadequate as a teacher. I realize now that teaching is similar to acting—the role requires a constant, high energy level. Once caught up by the role, I empathized—and tired easily."

—Kim Dunster, Stanford student

*"I wasn't gonna write nothin' for that class. But Kim convinced me
I should write."*

—Bonnie

Kim and Mark and the five other Stanford students who taught
this summer never felt completely at ease. They didn't really think
that we would ask them to be responsible for an entire class. During
the school year, as students in the Voice Project, they were able to
remain fairly passive. Teaching one or two days a week in the local
schools was fun. There were ideas from their own Voice Project
classes which they could use and enough time for preparation. The
abundance of time and fresh ideas was now gone. And so was the
room full of white, middle-class students.

They were bruised by student criticism. "Kim, you're sweet and
well-meaning." "Mark acts like a king on a pin cushion." And yet
they never gave up. At times Mark became negative and Kim would
become silent, but we all believed that any failure in a class session
was our fault. If Jackie was asleep, our boredom had put him there.
If David was at school and yet refused to come to class, it was our
inability to attract and hold his enthusiasm that was to blame. If
Lynn refused to write and sulked around the class, it was because,
as she said to me, "You don' wanna know me."

In the classroom the Stanford freshmen often lacked patience
and the tolerance for silence which is particularly necessary when
teaching students who have learned not to like school or teachers.
At times they couldn't accept the clatter and confusion that comes
with eleven students who have just discovered something worth
writing and talking about. We had to have three teachers in that
room just to keep up with all the side conversations, the shouted
questions, and the softly murmured discoveries. The hundreds of
hours they shared with the College of San Mateo students surely
accounts for part of the immense growth in self-confidence and
individual pride and the increasing willingness to write, which I
witnessed in these black students. I believe in the end we were all
colleagues.

At the end of the summer, Kim wrote to me:

"I have to write something about this summer."

"What are you goin' to write about?" He cooed it, laughing softly. "Write about how a nice white Stanford girl like you spent a nice, interesting summer teaching some poor ghetto Negroes how to write English."

"Lee, come on, not like that. That's unfair."

"Yeah, I know. I understand."

"It wasn't like that, Lee. I do not intend to reduce—or glorify—this past summer's work to that. I learned as much as you did, maybe more. And I walked in blind."

Without "reducing or glorifying" the summer, I too can say with certainty that it was always difficult. Our successes were never continuous or consistent. Student interest and participation were always fluctuating. The zeal and imagination of the teachers (freshmen and graduate students alike) were not always equal to the task of teaching. But what follows is an account of four successive classes held during the fifth week, a week in which we all learned together.[*]

"Games are fun. Now make up one that can teach somebody something."

At the end of the fourth week of our summer program Kim, Mark, and I were beginning to despair. We were unable to maintain the occasional high points of a class discussion from one day to another. And it seemed that we were running out of new ideas for teaching. Probably more than anything else, we were scared. We were out of ideas because there were no more ideas to be borrowed from other teachers who had used them in other situations. We had to create something for that class, for us, and for those students.

Over one weekend I worked on setting up a word or language game for Monday's class. "Games are fun. Now make up one that can teach somebody something," I said to myself on Saturday morning. On Sunday evening when Mark and Kim came over to plan for

[*] Dialogue appears exactly as it occurred. Words which seem to be omitted or misspelled are not transcription or typographical errors.

class I was prepared. "If I gave you a list of characters and person-alities and a set of quotations, could you match them up? Would it catch your attention even for a few minutes?" They were dubious, at best, about me and the game. "Games are phony. What happens after they get the right answer?" "What are we really trying to accomplish?" "This just keeps them away from the hard work of writing and that's why they'll like it." My reply was vague. "Well, we could make them tell us why they thought it was one person as opposed to another. Then they could read the quotes and maybe talk in the accent or dialect of the character. And maybe we could ask them to write a few more lines in that same person's voice." So we agreed to try it.

And within ten minutes, we were sprawled all over the floor in my living room rummaging through plays, novels, and short stories looking for voices. "Ahh, listen to this." "Does this sound like a college professor to you?" "God, they'll never get this one." By class time we had a list of fifteen characters and eleven quotations. We divided the class into three groups of four and each of us took a group, a tape recorder, and our game off to a separate corner of the campus.

I passed out the lists and we spent a few minutes reading over the quotations, and a couple of students began guessing out loud who the speakers were.

76-year-old rural widow
U.S. fighter pilot
Southern minister
Businessman
Treasurer of the American
    Dental Association
High School Principal
Ronald Reagan

7-year-old girl
White son of
    a southern U.S. Senator
New York taxi driver
LBJ
Chairman of small college English
    Department
Unemployed, 21-year-old Negro
42-year-old suburban housewife

1. So when I draw the Lord He'll be a real big man. He has to be to explain about the way things are.

2. Your education has been planned and geared to arm and prepare you to function as mature and thinking citizens capable of shouldering the burdens and responsibilities which a thriving democracy imposes.

3. Doorstep's dirty, why don't you take the chair there? I'd go look for him but I just got over my sciatica, and the fields are more than is ripe for me just now.

4. We takes the Bible at its word, and goes off on our own kind of original praying.

TOM: Who is talking in #1?

(*Long silence*)

TOM: Look at the words. Do they give you any clues?

(*Long silence*)

TOM: Who draws? Do any of you draw? Who would be talking about drawing?

(*Long silence*)

TOM: What's the Lord look like, Frances?

FRANCES: I don't know. I don't think you can see him.

TOM: Did you ever think he could be seen? I mean, did you used to?

FRANCES: When I went to Sunday School I had books with his picture in them.

DAVID: Aw, yeah, man. He had long hair and a robe and a beard.

TOM: Do you believe that now, David?

DAVID: Hell no, man.

TOM: All right then, what's that tell you about who might be talking here?

All during the discussion here there was a feverish attempt to match up the quote with a speaker. People were whispering to each other, laughing at their guesses, yelling out their matches, and ridiculing the other members of the class. I let them go until Bonnie shouted out, "It's the seven-year-old girl."

TOM: Why do you think so, Bonnie?

GWEN: 'Cause kids draw, 'specially in Sunday School, and they always think the Lord is big.

(*Loud approval from class, shouting and giggling*)

SKIP: A seven-year-old girl wouldn't use the word "explain."

TOM: Why not, Skip?

SKIP: It's too big. It sounds like you talkin'.

TOM: How would a seven-year-old say it then?

SKIP: He has to be to— He has to— He has to be to— That sounds like a kid there. But. He has to be to say way things are. He has to be to say the way things are.

FRANCES: Or, "he's gotta be to explain the way things are."

TOM: Does anyone want to guess what the girl would say next?

(*No one wanted to*)

SKIP: " 'Cause things sure are messed up." That's what I think she'd say.

After a short pause one of those things happened which seemed to take place all of the time this summer. Someone said, "Let's go to #2," and everyone started shouting "Yeah, yeah" as if they had the sure answer to #2. And they did. Everyone knew that that person speaking was a high school principal.

TOM: All right, then, let's read it the way we think it is spoken by this guy.

(*No one was eager to read, but I ignored them and said that I was going to read also, "so let's go."*)

Everyone read in a monotone as if the words were coming across a viewfinder. I tried to give it feeling. We recorded each reading and then played them back all together.

TOM: Which did you think sounded most like the principal?

SKIP: Mine.

TOM: Why?

SKIP: 'Cause it sounded like I wanted it to sound.

DAVID: No, Skip, you're wrong.

SKIP: Look, I know how I wanted it to sound.

TOM: Have you ever had a principal talk to you like that?

SKIP: Yep, Mr. _____ talks like that.

DAVID: No he don't. He talk real sof'.

SKIP: I can't help it.

FRANCES: But you gotta help it. You can't make him sound like you if you aren't him.

TOM: I thought mine was the best reading.

DAVID: Yeah, man, me too. That's what I thought.

TOM: Why?

DAVID: 'Cause your voice moved up and down.

FRANCES: You gave it emphasis.

BONNIE: You sounded like you'd been around a tape recorder all your life.

TOM: You mean you would sound different if there were no tape recorder?

BONNIE: No. (*Silence*) You just sound cultured.

We then went to #3 and Frances immediately said it was a seventy-six-year-old rural widow.

TOM: Why, Frances?

SKIP: That don't make no sense to me. . . . "why don't you take the chair?"

FRANCES: Well, the words "fields" and "ripe" make me think it is in the country. So it's rural.

TOM: Is that what gave you the key to it? Does the person speaking in #3 sound like a woman? A country woman?

SKIP: Sounds like a crazy woman.

TOM: Read it like an old woman, Frances.

FRANCES: I don't know how to read like an ol' woman.

TOM: Be old.

FRANCES: Uhhh . . . (*She then read it, but was interrupted in the second sentence.*)

DAVID: Naw, Frances.

FRANCES: I don't know how to read like an old woman.

(*Skip then read the first sentence and said he was confused.*)

SKIP: What's that mean? That's why I think she's crazy.

TOM: Okay. That sentence doesn't make perfect sense to you. You've noticed that. What would you want to say there? Add some words if you want to. Just make it clearer.

SKIP: *The* doorstep *is* dirty *so* why don't you take *that* chair *over* there?

(*The italicized words are his additions.*)

TOM: But this person is not talking that way.

DAVID: (*Imitating*) "Doorstep's dirty, why don't you take the chair over there?"

FRANCES: You put a word in, David.

SKIP: Maybe an old lady would say it like this—or she would leave out words.

FRANCES: Maybe she'll forget about it. 'Cause she's old.

TOM: Well, read it, Frances, the way you think it sounds. I bet you can make it sound natural for an old woman.

FRANCES: Aw no I can't read like a old woman.

TOM: Can you make any sense out of that phrase "and the fields are more than is ripe for me just now"?

SKIP: Means they are harvesting or it's too hot out there now.

FRANCES: I know what she means but maybe she says it that way because she is from the country.

TOM: How do people in the country talk?

DAVID: (*Imitating*) "You go on off over there." "Hey, boy."

TOM: Is there a difference between city and country people?

FRANCES: They say, "You all," and "Hey there."

TOM: I say, "You all."

SKIP: They say "go outdoors" instead of "outside."

DAVID: It don't sound right to me, man. I got to add a word to make it right.

TOM: Let me try reading it. (*I read it.*)

FRANCES: You sound like a old lady, too.

TOM: Okay. It's starting to make sense isn't it? It's almost natural. But there are things about it which seem wrong or strange to us. Like the way Skip said it is probably the way I would say it. But that isn't the way this writer has this person speaking. If I ask you to write like a seventy-six-year-old woman, do you think you would be able to write something like the way this person sounds? Can you give a person a voice when you write that makes them sound like they really are? Or would you make a seventy-six-year-old woman sound more like yourselves?

BONNIE: I could do it.

TOM: Who would be the easiest person for you to give voice to?

BONNIE: I don' know. I never thought about that. I don' know.

DAVID: Not really. (*Giggling*)

TOM: Can you imitate a coach?

DAVID: No.

TOM: Then you tell me how your basketball coach speaks. Tell me what is different about the way you speak in regard to the way he speaks.

DAVID: I speak soft and he yells a lot.

TOM: Does he yell a lot?

DAVID: Yeah. (*Then in a soft restrained voice*) "Goddam your ass. Let's get it."

TOM: Great! Go on. I want to hear more from him and less from you.

DAVID: (*His voice increasing in pitch*) "You're tired, hunh, get off your ass and fix it."

SKIP: Yeah, he says "You guys" and "Git" a lot. He has an accent but ah—it's not an accent only—I don't know how to say it. From the words a colored person would use and a white person would use. They might be the same but they sound different.

TOM: Can you put a sound in writing?

BONNIE: Yeah. If they was country you could put "ain't" and stuff like that in there.

SKIP: I don't mean a country accent.

TOM: How about spelling? That can make different sounds. Take the "get." I want to get a car today. How do you spell "get"?

BONNIE: G-e-t.

TOM: Now you want to make that sound like a country boy and you say, "Ah'm goin' to git me a new cah today." How would you spell "get"?

FRANCES: G-i-t.

TOM: Right. And when you read it you couldn't mistake it for g-e-t.

BONNIE: But you'd try to read it as "get" . . . if you were reading it as a book.

TOM: Don't you let yourself hear the voices when you read, Bonnie? For instance, if you were from the country would you say, "I am not going to git me a car today"?

FRANCES: No, you'd say, "I ain't."

DAVID: Or "I isn't."

TOM: What is the difference between "I am" and "I is"?

SKIP: The words are different but there is no difference in meaning.

TOM: There's no difference in meaning!

SKIP: They's both going to get the car.

TOM: Who is "they"? Are "they" the same?

SKIP: No—they mean the same thing. But they said it with different words. And we know that one of 'em doesn't speak right.

We then went on to #4.

TOM: Who is speaking in #4?

SKIP: (*Reading*) He takes the Bible . . .

BONNIE: A southern Negro minister.

TOM: Why do you think that is so, Bonnie?

BONNIE: 'Cause he sounds southern.

TOM: What in there sounds southern?

SKIP: "Goes."

TOM: What's wrong with that?

SKIP: It should be just plain "go."

TOM: Should be?

SKIP: That's the way I'd say it. (*He then reads the sentence the way he prefers it. But in the reading he also leaves off the "s" in "takes."*)

TOM: Okay, Skip, read that first phrase again.

SKIP: (*Reading*) "We take the Bible . . ."

TOM: What did you just do? Read it again.

SKIP: "We take the Bible . . ."

TOM: You aren't reading it the way it's written.

SKIP: Well, that's the way I say it.

DAVID: That ain't the way it's written, bub.

TOM: Why can't you read it the way it's written, Skip?

SKIP: I don't talk that way. That's the way this man talks. Not me.

TOM: What about the phrase "our own kind of original praying"? Can you make that sound more like a northern minister or church?

FRANCES: (*After long silence*) "Personal kind of prayer."

DAVID: Or "unique form of praying."

TOM: The word "praying" sounds too country to me. I see that minister up there shouting and screaming and telling everyone to begin praying and by gawd they sure enough commence. Can you see that? (*Laughter is out of control. Skip is up walking around the table and telling David he's never seen anyone so gassed over words before.*) And in that nice quiet city church in New York, the minister raises his hands, invokes the Lord's benevolence, and speaks out the Lord's Prayer by himself. Skippy, read that the way a southern minister or preacher would say it.

He reads the sentence and then we listen to it on the tape recorder. Bonnie reads it and we listen to her.

TOM: Bonnie, did you act it out?

SKIP: She didn't even read it the way it was on there.

BONNIE: I did too.

SKIP: You said, "We take the Bible . . ."

BONNIE: Oh— "We takes the Bible"—I just can't say that—Sorry.

TOM: Of course—That's all I want you to see. It's hard for me to say it that way, too.

DAVID: Yeah, it is man.

TOM: In writing you might have to write about other people, and other places, and other things. So how do you do it? Well, one of the ways is to start getting in their bag. Ooops, that's just what I did. "Bag" is your word, see, not mine. Why don't you read it, Frances.

FRANCES: "We takes the Bible at its own word—"

TOM: Its what kind of word?

FRANCES: "At its own word"—oh, "at its word."

TOM: Why do you keep adding words?

FRANCES: 'Cause it doesn't sound right.

TOM: For you it doesn't. But how about a southern minister?

FRANCES: Oh, it's perfect for him.

TOM: Well, you have just heard a voice that is not your own. A voice so different from yours that you have trouble duplicating it.

David asked to read it again. He has tremendous difficulty reading and so I went through the sentence with him one word at a time. Then he read it without much halting and stammering. We listened to a recording of his reading and when it was over he let out a huge sigh and asked to read it with feeling now that he had gotten the words down. The next recording was so good the other kids in the class clapped for him.

After class David asked if we could do this "same sort of stuff" tomorrow. He suggested that he could run the tape recorder which would free me so I "could do more teaching and acting." That evening, however, David was arrested for some offense and didn't get back to our class with any regularity or enthusiasm for the rest of the summer.

For our next meeting we prepared another list of quotations and possible speakers. Our hope for this class was to have the students write additional passages in the voice of the speaker once they had identified him and duplicated the sound of his speech. To make this more likely we chose longer quotations.

TOM: Does anyone know if David is here today?

BONNIE: He's in court this morning.

TOM: Will he be coming to class?

BONNIE: I don't think so.

TOM: Well . . . Uh. I've drawn up another list for you this morning and it's a little more difficult than yesterday's. The speeches are a little longer and they may be harder to identify—but you'll know more about the speaker this way and you should even be

able to write in his voice by the time we are finished. So let's
take a look at #1:

> They was all drunk, and when they seen your father's brother
> they let out a great whoop and holler and they aimed the car
> straight at him, the way they do sometimes, you know. But they
> was drunk. And I guess the boy, being drunk, too, and scared, kind
> of lost his head. By the time he jumped it was too late. And, time
> your father got down the hill, his brother weren't nothing but blood
> and pulp.

After a few minutes we all read the passage aloud so that everyone could understand the words.

TOM: Who is speaking here?

SKIP: Sounds like a good old boy [a southern redneck].

TOM: Why do you say that, Skip?

SKIP: Well, 'cause they was all drunk and whoopin' and hollerin'.
And they left that man in bloody. Sounds like that's what a good
old boy would do.

TOM: Do you all agree with Skip?

FRANCES: I don't know . . . what he said I agree with, but that
"your father" bit doesn't fit.

TOM: Huh?

FRANCES: I mean it sounds like someone is talking or telling a story
to someone else. And it wouldn't be a good old boy telling it,
would it?

BONNIE: I think it's a story about good old boys. But this person
isn't one of them.

TOM: Now some of you have said it is a story. Is that what it is
or is it a speech to an audience or just a person thinking to
himself?

FRANCES: No, it's got to be a story . . . from one person to another.

TOM: What makes you think so, Frances?

FRANCES: It just sounds like a conversation to me.

(*Long silence*)

TOM: Is that a man or woman speaking?

FRANCES: I think it is a woman. . . . see the way she says "the boy

being drunk, too, and scared, . . ." —it's like she feels sorry for
him or doesn't want to blame him.

SKIP: Naw, naw. No woman would say "blood and pulp."

TOM: What do you mean?

SKIP: It just doesn't sound right for a girl to say it that way. She
would say something like, "and his brother was dead."

BONNIE: Well, I think it's a woman.

TOM: Well there are only two women on the list. Which one is it?

BONNIE: The elderly Negro mother.

TOM: Why couldn't it be the social worker? Couldn't she be telling
a family about the death of a relative?

FRANCES: I don't think so. My social worker doesn't talk that way.
She uses such big words I just look into her mouth and leave
the house.

BONNIE: Yeah, that's right.

TOM: Okay, tell me how she sounds like an elderly Negro mother.
What clues do you get in this passage?

SKIP: Her talk isn't right. Down there where she says, "his brother
weren't nothing . . ." It sounds wrong.

TOM: How should it be?

SKIP: Umm . . . "his brother were—his brother was nothing but
blood and pulp."

BONNIE: That's better.

TOM: Look at the end of that first sentence. ". . . and they aimed the
car straight at him, the way they do sometimes, you know." And
she goes on, "And I guess the boy, being drunk, too, and scared,
kind of lost his head." What does that sound like? What do all
those commas do in those sentences?

SKIP: She can't make up her mind.

TOM: Haven't you heard old people sort of keep adding words and
phrases while they're talking, like the ideas are a little slow in
coming?

FRANCES: My mother talks that way sometimes. It's almost like a
philosopher.

TOM: Wow, that's right! It's like they have seen all the world and
can account for it all of the time. So they add little things in a

sentence which will help to explain something, without saying that's what they are doing.

I explained that the passage was from James Baldwin's story, "Sonny's Blues," and is, in fact, a mother telling her son a story. I then asked them to read the passage over a few more times, both aloud and to themselves, and then write the next few sentences that the mother would speak. To do this, they would have to capture her voice and the purpose of the story she was telling. The students' written responses are listed below. They read their writing into the tape recorder and then we discussed each of the pieces.

> Your father kneeled down beside his brother and began to cry and curse the boys in the car.
>
> —Skip

SKIP: I thought it was good except for the last part. I didn't know how to end it.

TOM: The word "curse" bothered me a little. But I bet that mother wouldn't use the word "swore" either. She'd probably use a softer word than "swear." But I'm not sure that she would feel comfortable with "curse."

SKIP: She shouldn't say "curse" and she wouldn't say "swore." She'd say, uh, "cuss." And I think I'd make it "them boys" 'stead of "the boys." It's too gentle.

> And there was nothing your father could do but cry for his dead brother. And that's why I'm telling you not to drive when you're drunk because it can happen to you as well as to your father.
>
> —Bonnie

TOM: You gave a reason for the conversation. What was your first sentence again? (*Bonnie reads it.*) That's interesting. Both you and Skip have this man crying over his brother. Do you think— How did you like the moral at the end? Do you think that is the reason the mother was talking to the boy?

SKIP: Well, I thought she was telling the boy about his uncle.

TOM: Why does this mother sound so serious? Is she talking about the uncle?

FRANCES: I guess she's tryin' to get the boy to understand his father more.

TOM: Right! The focus is upon the father, not the person who dies. So that when you write, "and there was nothing the father could do but cry," or "Your father kneeled down beside his brother and cried," you are carrying out the emphasis of the speaker—that mother.

> All he could do was stand there and look at the mess and try to understand what had happened and why. He had tears in his eyes and anger on his face.
>
> —Frances

TOM: How did you like that, Bonnie?

BONNIE: I liked it.

SKIP: The last sentence was the best.

TOM: How does the word "mess" sound to you?

FRANCES: Well, there's nothing left, ya know, but blood and pulp, flesh and bone. I think that's a mess.

(*Frances reads her passage again out loud.*)

SKIP: When she says "why" the father is the center. That's good.

TOM: Which of the three do you like the best?

FRANCES: They're all good.

TOM: Would you like to continue this sort of thing tomorrow?

SKIP: I'd like to do a play with parts.

TOM: Would one of you direct it?

FRANCES: Skippy could.

SKIP: What'd ya mean, direct?

TOM: Well, like, if someone has a line and they don't say it the right way, you tell them how to say it.

SKIP: Oh, yeah.

TOM: What I've been concerned about here is realizing through writing and reading and speaking that there are other people in the world. And that they are people very different from yourselves. Not only are they different because of the way they look, or where they come from, or their sex, or how old they are, but they are different because of the way they talk and the way they sound. In writing you can really bring out those differences and you can identify the person by the way he talks. That's what we mean by voice. In two more weeks, by the end of this summer, I'll get a piece of writing, and hand it out to the class and you're going to be able to say, *that's* Frances Earle or *that's* Bonnie Drayton. People are going to be able to recognize you by what you write and how you write it. And vice versa, if you want to write about an ice cream vendor, someone is going to read it and say, by god, that guy sounds like he sells ice cream on the streets of Brooklyn.

The following day I brought in a selection from *The Invisible Man*, by Ralph Ellison. I converted the passage from an extended dialogue into a short play with three speakers:

Trueblood: I couldn't even let go when I heard Kate scream. It was a scream to make your blood run cold. It sounds like a woman who was watchin' a team of wild horses run down her baby chile and she caint move. Kate's hair is standin' up like she done seen a ghost, her gown is hanging open and the veins in her neck is 'bout to bust. And her eyes! Lawd, them eyes. I'm lookin' up at her from where I'm layin on the pallet with Matty Lou, and I'm too weak to move. She screams and starts to pickin' up the first thing that comes to her hand and throwin it. Some of them misses me and some of them hits me. Little things and big things. Somethin' cold and strong-stinkin' hits me and wets me and bangs against my head. Somethin' hits the wall—boom-a-loom-a-loom!—like a cannon ball, and I tries to cover up my head. Kate's talkin' the unknown tongue, like a wild woman.

T-2: Wait a minit, Kate. Stop it!

Trueblood: Then I hears her stop a second and I hears her runnin' across the floor, and I twists and looks and Lawd, she done got my double-barrel shotgun! And while she's foamin' at the mouth and cockin' the gun she gits her speech.

Kate: Git up! Git up!

T-2: HEY! NAW! KATE!

Kate: Goddam yo' soul to hell! Git up offa my chile!

T-2: But woman, Kate, lissen.

Kate: Don't talk, MOVE!

T-2: Down that thing, Kate!

Kate: No down, UP!

T-2: That there's buckshot, woman, BUCKshot!

Kate: Yes, it is!

T-2: Down it, I say!

Kate: I'm gon blast your soul to hell!

T-2: You gon hit Matty Lou!

Kate: Not Matty Lou—YOU!

T-2: It spreads, Kate. Matty Lou!

Trueblood: She moves around, aimin' at me.

Kate: I done warn you, Jim.

T-2: Kate, it was a dream. Lissen to me.

Kate: You the one who lissen—UP FROM THERE!

Trueblood: She jerks the gun and I shuts my eyes. But insteada thunder and lightin' bustin' me, I hears Matty Lou scream in my ear. And when I looks up, Maan, Maan! she's got a iron in her hand!

T-2: No blood, Kate. Don't spill no blood!

Kate: You low-down dog, it's better to spill than to foul.

T-2: Naw, Kate. Things ain't what they 'pear! Don't make no blood-sin on accounta no dream-sin!

Kate: Shut up, nigguh. You done fouled!

TOM: Let's see if we can act this thing out. Trouble is, Trueblood's a man, and T-2 is a man.

(*Frances reads it with much imitation and drama.*)

TOM: Can I interrupt you, Frances?

FRANCES: Yeah.

TOM: How come you're reading it like that?

FRANCES: I was just playin'. (*Laughing*)

TOM: Playin'? But that's just about the way that guy sounds, isn't it? You weren't reading it: (*In monotone*) Now I heard Frances Earle read that way (*in a monotone*) about two weeks ago. I even heard her read that way yesterday.

FRANCES: When?—two weeks ago? When'd you hear me read like that?

TOM: You've read like that—everybody's read like that since the course started. Right? And you did it two days ago. But you just picked this thing up and you started—Read it again like you just read it. Play. Okay, I don't care if you call it "play."

(*She reads it again.*)

TOM: Okay, who is T-2? Who is the next person speaking?

BONNIE: A man.

TOM: Okay, I shouldn't have put T-2, but can you guess who that is?

BONNIE: Trueblood.

TOM: Yeah, that's right. Now why would I put T-2?

BONNIE: To abbreviate, I guess.

TOM: Okay, but why the "2"? Why the number?

FRANCES: I don't know.

BONNIE: Why would you put T-2 here and Trueblood—

TOM: If T-2 is also Trueblood—Is he doing something different when I have T-2 in front of what he says?

BONNIE: Um. I think so.

TOM: Can you guess what it is?

BONNIE: Like "Wait a minute, Kate, stop it." Maybe that's—that one right there maybe he's yelling or—

TOM: He's yelling it. He's saying it, isn't he? All right, in that paragraph that Frances just read, what's he doing?

FRANCES: Layin' in the porch, getting all beat up, getting throwed at.

TOM: But what's he doing in his speech?

FRANCES: Nothing.

TOM: What kind of a speech would you say that is?

FRANCES: He's telling what's happening—

BONNIE: He's not hollering or anything.

TOM: Not hollering. But he's telling what's happening, isn't he? He's describing, he's setting the scene, he's painting a picture telling a story. Then in that second thing where he says, "Wait a minute, Kate, stop it!" he's in that story, he's doin' something . . . What's happening is that this guy is telling a story. Trueblood is telling a story to two people. And as he tells the story, every once in a while he comes to a point where he says what he said in the situation that he's describing. . . . I'm going to tell you a story about buying a car: Frances and Bonnie, I went down to a used car lot yesterday in San Mateo County and I was looking for a used Volkswagen. And it was a hot day, and there weren't many salesmen around, but finally I got somebody's attention, and I said to him, "Mr. Smith, I'm lookin' for a used Volkswagen, about a 1960, 1965."—See what's happening there? What were the two things I just did in speech?

FRANCES: You told us about what was happening, what you did yesterday.

TOM: And then I did what?

FRANCES: And then you started talking to the salesman.

TOM: Right. And the first Trueblood is the guy telling the story. T-2 is also Trueblood, but it's Trueblood in the story. Now, the author does this. Let me read to you from Ralph Ellison's book called *The Invisible Man.*

(*I read a short passage.*)

BONNIE: Is this a Negro or a white?

TOM: Who do you think it is? (*Long silence*)

BONNIE: Sounds black to me.

FRANCES: Sounds like somebody from the South—Matty Lou.

TOM: Does that sound like a southern name?

FRANCES: Yeah—Matty Lou. . . .

TOM: Now, Bonnie says it sounds like a Negro. Why does it sound like a Negro to you, Bonnie?

BONNIE: 'Cause—you know, some of 'em, they haven't had much schooling. It sounds just like—"Lawd, them eyes." You know, somebody that goes to church all the time, you know, is gonna say "Lawd"— (*Laughing*) And all that stuff.

TOM: Yeah, and look at the fourth line, how she pronounces "cannot," or "can't."

BONNIE: "Caint."

TOM: "Caint." Remember how the other day we were talking about if I was a city boy and I said I was going to get me a car. How would you spell "get"?

BONNIE: G-e-t.

TOM: And if I was a country boy and I said, "I'm going down the country and git me a woman."

BONNIE: G-i-t.

TOM: And that's one of the ways you can tell something about the

language and something about people. And look here, look how
he spelled "can't." How's he spell it?

BONNIE: C-a-i-n-t.

TOM: Now one of the things is that when you read it—let's say you
read it silently. You don't have to read it in front of a tape recorder. One of the things you know immediately is, that person
isn't educated, or that person is speaking in a certain sort of way.
But when you read it out loud, not only is it misspelled, but it
sounds a certain way. And when you hear it sounded out—
"caint"—you force yourself to listen to it. And then you see it.
And you see what that person's done with his speech. And this
writer is not trying to cover that fact up. In fact, he's really
emphasizing it. He wants you to know something about that person who's speaking. Let's act this thing out.

(*Reading. Frances is Trueblood, Bonnie is Kate, and Mark, a
Stanford student, is T-2.*)

TOM: Do you know what's happening?

BONNIE: (*Laughing loudly, almost crying*) What's happening?

TOM: What do you think it means when she says, "You done
fouled"?

BONNIE: You have messed up.

TOM: Yeah, that's right. How do you think he's messed up?

FRANCES: He just went out with her daughter.

BONNIE: (*Laughing*) He slept with her daughter. . . . Oh, what a
play! Oh God.

GWEN: (Another CSM student who comes to our table out of curiosity) Where you get this at?

TOM: It's out of this book, Gwen. Finally she hits him with the ax,
right across the head. Doesn't kill him, but it sure does tear him
up. All right Bonnie, you ought to do it again. I know you can get
better than that—and Mark—

GWEN: Mark is too polite!

TOM: (*Laughing*) All right, coach Mark. What's wrong with it?
What's he doing?

FRANCES: Gotta put the feeling into it. (*Laughing*)

GWEN: Was that you who was reading it all along?

TOM: Yeah—Well, he was just reading the T-2 part. Why didn't Mark sound like he was alive to you?

BONNIE: 'Cause—he was talkin' like Mark. I mean he talked like he was regular talkin'—"Hey, naw, Kate," that's what he said.

TOM: How should he have said it?

BONNIE: "Hey, naw, Kate." (Shouting)

TOM: He's saying "no"—"Hey *naw!* Kate!" She's comin' with this goddam shotgun sayin' "Git up, git up!"—"Hey naw, Kate!" (Laughter) "Git up off my chile!"

BONNIE: You do it so good! (Laughing)

TOM: It's not that Mark's just talking too much like himself, but Frances, who's reading and telling this story, is reading with more expression than T-2.

GWEN: You really are!

TOM: All right, Gwen, I want to read a part. You want to read a part?

GWEN: No. (Softly)

FRANCES: Yeah! Git it!

GWEN: I can't.

FRANCES: Be Kate. You can't?

TOM (Singsong) She can't say, "Shut up, nigger." (Laughter)

FRANCES: Go on.

TOM: I'll be Trueblood. Bonnie, you be T-2.

GWEN: I can't do this.

FRANCES: Speak. Forget yourself.

GWEN: How do you sound like you come from a—

FRANCES: "You all" and—

TOM: Oh yeah, Kate's Trueblood's wife, and he is a tenant sharecropper, Negro tenant sharecropper in—

BONNIE: Kate's wife?

TOM: Kate is Trueblood's wife.

BONNIE: And Matty Lou is the daughter.

TOM: Yeah. So what you want to sound like is a forty-year-old Negro woman, who's married to a rural farmer, sharecropper, very poor Negro, and you just woke up in a dingy old cabin and find your husband sittin' on top of your daughter. He isn't exactly sittin', either. (*Laughing*)

GWEN: Well, that must be her stepfather, then, right?

BONNIE: We don't know. I don't know. (*Bonnie answers with the voice of a young English teacher. She sounded so professional it scared me.*)

GWEN: "Git up. Git up." I can't—(*Starts to read Kate's part and stops*)

TOM: Okay, go ahead and read it and we'll listen to it afterwards and you can see what you didn't quite do. Go ahead.
(*Reading*)

TOM: You turned into a real bitch in the middle of that, Gwen. (*Laughter*) But you know, the last thing that you said—you said "Shut up, nigger, you done foul." That last sentence—you didn't keep it up.—God, that's good, Gwen. Hey, I got an idea for tomorrow. . . .

My idea was to have these three students produce and direct the reading of this passage with the other students in the larger class. They were excited about the possibility and directed the entire class by themselves. I played back the tape of the above class and let them hear themselves coaching each other on the various parts. And the following day they were able to do the same thing without any direction from the Stanford teachers.

Two days later, after the entire class had read and acted out the section from *The Invisible Man,* we wrote the following words on the blackboard: Mamma, ooooo, MAMA! This was the scream of Matty Lou's which I had deleted from the original dialogue. Now we were going to use it as the basis of a writing assignment. We discussed the sound of the scream, the way that Ellison had written the three words to give them emphasis and feeling, and the possibilities of learning about Matty Lou just from this one scream. Then we asked each of them to write a few sentences in the voice of Matty Lou, describing her feelings, or saying what she would say in this situation.

The writing was done in class and then each student read his piece for the class. Each was recorded and played back for the writer. They were hesitant at first but before the class was over all of the students had read.

LYNNE: Well, you read yours. That's what you should do.
TOM: I believe you're next in line.
LYNNE: No, I'm not. No, no, no.
PAT: Go on read yours, Lynne—
LYNNE: I don't have one.
TOM: What's that?
KIM: What's this?
LYNNE: That's a hunk o' junk.
PAT: "Hunk o' junk." Go ahead!
TOM: You read yours first.
LYNNE: No.
PAT: Lynne, go along with the game, now—read yours first.
TOM: Okay. I will read.

> Mama! Oooooo mama! Daddy did done gone crazy an' is tryin' to get me. [*Laughter*—"*shhhh*"] Stop Daddy! Please git up off me! Mama, he's a hurtin!—stop him—knock him off!
>
> —Tom

(*Much laughter*)
TOM: Why are you all screamin!? (*More laughter*) You don't think I should say that?
GWEN: Uh uh.
TOM: Okay, why not?
BONNIE: Like "knock him off"—What'd you say?
TOM: I said: "Mama, Ooooo mama, Daddy did done gone crazy an' is tryin' to git me. Stop, Daddy! Please git up off me." I don't like that.
PAT: I wouldn't say "please." She shouldn't say "please." She should be havin' fits—
TOM: But it is her daddy.
PAT: Yeah, I know it's her daddy—

GWEN: But you still wouldn't say "please."

TOM: Okay.

PAT: —an' "knock him off"—

TOM: "Mama, he's hurtin'. Stop him. Knock him off." . . . Well? Now she said "please," and you think that's too polite, and you think "knock him off" is too strong? What would she say?

PAT: Probably somethin' like— I don't want to read this. I don't know. But I know she wouldn't say—you know.

TOM: Yeah, well, what I was trying to do—first of all she says, "Daddy did done gone crazy an' is tryin' to git me." And she sorta screams that out into the room. And then she looks at her daddy, and she says, "Stop Daddy! Please git up off me!" She's sort of pleading with him. And finally you know, "Mama, he's hurtin'. Stop him, knock him off," anything, just get him away. That's the way I thought of it.

FRANCES: Why'd you think of that?

TOM: What—(*Laughter*) What'd you think of it, Lynne? What were you all giggling and getting up and messing around for?

LYNNE: I was thinkin' it.

TOM: You mean it wasn't any good?

GIRLS: GOOD!

Listed below are a few more examples of the students' writing for this assignment. Each of them is reproduced exactly as it was written. The class caught the tension of the situation and in writing rendered it in the excited, halting, and alarmed voice of Matty Lou. They gave speech to a personality. As each student read his passage, the emotion of the scene was captured with inflection and intensity and rhythm. The control of grammar and spelling has heightened the reality of the speaker and the content of the speech.

Ahhh shit, Trueblood, if you don't get your big ass off me. Mama, git this nigguh off a me!

—Pat

I'm awakened by my father bein' pulled off by my mother. I run and I'm a standin' by Daddy. I'm as stiff as a log. Mama cussin' an' a hittin'. Mama picks up a buckshot an' aims at Daddy. I run

to the door screamin' "Mama, oooooo Mama." Still hollerin' I say,
"Mama, Lord Mama, what have Pa done?"

—Bonnie

Mama, Oooo Mama! Daddy, you dirty old man, get the hell off
a me! Mama, tell him to get the hell off a me. Damned if I sleep
on that old pallet with you all again. You better stop messin'
around with me and find you another girl. Mama, stop from that.
Mama, stop—now. Hit him with the axe! If I wasn't under him
I'd use it myself. You better go get you a five cents whore on the
corner an' lets me alone.

—Frances

These four classes reflect much of the scope and purpose of the
Voice Project during the summer and throughout the year. We
began by reading and listening to spoken passages in order to
identify the speaker. To do this we had to focus upon rhythm, word
choice, control of dialect and accent, and the sounds of language.
Then we moved to student imitations of other voices, both in
writing and speaking, in order to emphasize variations among characters and authors and people that we hear every day. The dramatic readings enabled students to experience the excitement of
words in speech as well as the power of capturing human dialogue
in writing. Writing a voice for a new character was the final extension of a process that moved from identification to reproduction
and imitation to creation. In the last week of the program we had
the students write their own speeches about topical issues. In this
exercise they moved closer to the possibility of creating and revealing their own personal writing voices.

8

The Untaught Teacher

DENISE LEVERTOV

Introductory

I came to teaching from the peculiar standpoint of one who has never been to school. As a child I "did lessons" at home under the tutelage of my mother and listened to the BBC Schools Programs. For French, piano, and art, I was sent to various teachers for private lessons. My only experience of classroom work was in ballet school, from the age of twelve through to seventeen; in a year of nursing school when I was twenty-one; and in a Russian language class I attended at the New School in New York a few years ago.

My experience of what it is like to be a student seemed to me, when I began to teach, to be a disability. I had plenty to say, plenty I was eager to impart if I could; but no models of procedure, no memories to draw on of how much a student could reasonably be expected to study in a given period of time. Afraid of boring my students, I talked too much and both bored and frustrated them. Work which they could have profitably done themselves—a kind of summary of each week's class (this was a poetry workshop at the N.Y. Poetry Center)—I did myself, in my uncertainty that I had really put across in the two-hour period all that I had intended to cram into it. But as time went by—both in that course and in my subsequent college teaching ventures—I came to see my inexperience as something of an advantage, even if it made things harder for me: it has meant that so far, at least, I have inevitably brought to teaching a freshness, a quality of improvisation, that I believe my students have found stimulating. Too many of them have been disillusioned by finding that a teacher has been using some familiar trickery upon them—professional gimmicks, fake spontaneity, ploys.

What the non-professional teacher—the artist who is invited to teach *his thing*—has to offer must surely be precisely a fresh response to the individual group of students and his passionate interest in the art he is teaching, free from habits picked up from his own former teachers or in courses on pedagogy. Obviously the gifted and dedicated professional teacher is not going to impose tricks on his students, either, if he can help it. But it must be difficult indeed for the professional, often overworked and perhaps longing for a Sabbatical, to avoid almost unconsciously reusing gambits which worked the year before, not to speak of old notes rehashed. The artist who is a part-time teacher, especially if like myself he has taught each year at a different school, can more easily, confronted not only with new faces but with a different style of student in each place, forget what he did last time, or if he remembers it, find it inappropriate to this new group and new surroundings, and so start out with a genuine sense of adventure; while if my peculiar lack of formal education has at times caused me to demand too much or too little of my students, it has at least helped me, I think, to recognize how much there was for me to learn from them and for them to learn from each other.

Poetry Center Workshop

My first teaching assignment, the course traditionally called The Craft of Poetry, has been taught at the Poetry Center of the Y.M.H.A. in New York by many different poets over the years. It is held in the evening, once a week for twelve weeks, and the teacher has the opportunity of seeing poems and statements by a very large number of applicants (fifty or sixty) well beforehand and limiting the number of students to what he considers the optimum for the kind of course he intends to teach—which is entirely his own decision. I chose twelve students, varying in age from seventeen to perhaps forty-six, though most of them were between perhaps twenty-three and thirty-five. At the last moment I took in a thirteenth; but with one student dropping out after the first few classes, and irregular attendance by some others, eight students became the regular core of the class. Several of these were already very accomplished poets.

My hope was not to teach anybody to write poetry—indeed I had deep suspicions of the very idea of poetry workshops—but to attempt to bring each one to a clearer sense of what his own voice and range might be and to give him some standards by which to evaluate his own work. My major emphasis was on the poem as a sonic entity, not fully experienced if not heard as well as seen; and so each poem under discussion was always read aloud—preferably several times, and by several persons as well as by its author—before we began to talk about it. There were usually mimeographed copies for everyone to scrutinize, though as the course progressed and people kept bringing in new poems this wasn't always successfully organized, and indeed many poems were mimeographed which we never had time to discuss. Each week I would prepare what amounted to a short lecture on some particular aspect of poetry, such as the use and abuse of rhyme, the function of the personal pronoun and its non-functional intrusion, the relation of form to content, and so forth, and try to find among the students' work a poem or poems that would aptly illustrate my point. This would take perhaps half the period, and the second half would usually be given to the reading and criticism of some other poems. In my over-anxiety, at that time, to keep control of the situation, I often maintained this structure perhaps too rigidly.

Assignments were few and consisted almost entirely of reading; writing assignments were confined to keeping a notebook which would include notes on the class, but these were "on trust" and I did not ask to see them. I wanted above all not to have anyone writing poems "for the class," forcing himself to write when he had nothing to say. My assumption was that if they were poets (and some most certainly were) they would write when they had to, and show me what they wished to show. If any one of them, though a poet, happened during part or all of those twelve weeks to be in a period of not writing, it was my hope that the general principles I was trying to formulate and instill would be of future use to him in any case; and I certainly didn't want any who turned out not to be poets at all to be artificially stimulated, by mere emulation and by assigned work, to a deceptive efflorescence, if I could help it. (This has remained a firm principle in my later teaching experience, though I have somewhat modified its application as I shall detail on a later page.) I myself, however, as I have already noted, was doing a good deal of homework. I used to rush back home each week and write my summary of the class—not only of what I had said or intended to say, but what everyone else had contributed too—plus axioms and apposite quotes from the Masters —from Pound, Rilke, William Carlos Williams, etc.—and from my own current reading. I would hurry this into the mail, to be mimeographed at the Poetry Center along with the week's batch of new poems for distribution at the next class. My idea was that even if the evening's discussion had become a muddle, each student would have at the end of the course a sort of little book of principles that he could go on using forever. Some of the students have assured me that they do indeed refer back to those summaries from time to time, and value them; but I myself later came to realize that I was spoon-feeding them. Because these were more mature people than the average college class and were for the most part not in need of prodding, some very fine work was written during the course; and when I began to sit back and listen to some of them discuss each other's poems I found myself learning that I did not have to undertake *all* the teaching—that they had as much to learn from each other as from me. Richard Lourie, for instance, often could put his finger on exactly what it was that was wrong in a poem about which I had only felt an unfocused dissatisfaction; or Emmett Jarrett would come to my aid with a knowledge of prosody far exceeding my own. (These are two young men whose work is beginning to become known since that time.)

Probably the most important benefit of the course for teacher and students alike was in the stimulation of each other's company and the still-continuing friendships that developed from our association in class.

Drew University

My next two teaching assignments were concurrent. Drew University, in New Jersey, asked me to teach a weekly poetry class along the same workshop lines as the one at the Poetry Center; and C.C.N.Y. invited me to become the non-resident equivalent of a "poet in residence." The two groups of students were quite dissimilar.

At Drew—a class of about fifteen students—attitudes or at any rate behavior tended to be, with one or two exceptions, trusting or even docile, with an expectation of being told what to do by the teacher; whereas my C.C.N.Y. students that first term were mistrustful of anyone over thirty, in typical big-city style. Drew students for the most part shared a middle-middle class, more or less suburban background—most frequently in New Jersey—and their ethnic origins were predominantly Anglo-Saxon. They were mostly sophomores and juniors, with one or two seniors and, I think, one freshman; there were a few more girls than boys. Once again I had had the opportunity of choosing among the applicants; but here there was neither a large number to choose from nor were there more than three or four whose pre-course work showed unmistakable talent. My greatest difficulty, during the first semester, was that I felt bored and exasperated at lengthy discussions of bad poems and yet did not know how to avoid them without utterly discouraging the beginners who had written them. The more talented and sophisticated students shared my boredom. But I had genuine liking and concern for each of these kids, and my pleasure in seeing whatever development took place in them during the year outweighed the frustrations.

I was under no illusions about how many of them might go on to write poetry of value after the year was over; but there is justification in such a class if—by writing even one or two poems that are not mere doggerel, on the one hand, or purely private "self-expressive" effusion, on the other, and by recognizing the shortcomings and achievements of others—each student becomes a better reader of poetry than he might otherwise have been. I believed my own enjoyment of paintings to derive some of its acuteness from my early attempts to be a painter myself; and it seemed reasonable to suppose that just as my memory of what it feels like to hold a brushful of paint or to see the need, in a composition, for a stronger line here and a lightening of tone there, enters into my appreciation of what a painter has done with his canvas, so a non-poet temporarily engaging with the process of writing a poem would retain forever something of an insider's view when reading, and thereby deepen his satisfaction and the intelligence with which he read.

The structure of each week's class was not very different from that of the Poetry Center classes the year before, but with the addition of several elements: the reading and discussion of poems by good poets of various periods (mainly modern, since, as in most colleges, the students' knowledge of twentieth-century poetry was poor)—so that they had something with which to contrast their own work; a good deal of emphasis on their learning to read aloud properly (God knows what speech departments do, if anything!—certainly the average American student has little concept even of how to produce his voice, not to speak of how to read a poem aloud); and a small but regular amount of assigned reading. Writing assignments did not consist of poetry but of notebooks. Since I didn't want to intrude on their privacy, I asked them to make these looseleaf notebooks, so that though I would periodically ask to see them, any personal revelations they did not wish me to read could be removed before they handed their books in. I believe notebooks to be perhaps the only sure and honest way a writer can stimulate his creativity—that is, can find out that he has more to write than he thought, as distinct from forcing himself to write when he has nothing to say. To be useful, they must not be either mere "backward engagement books" or the kind of lengthy self-analytic confessionals that become substitutes for living. A useful *writer's* notebook typically consists of brief descriptions (in prose) of things seen or heard; a word or phrase that is haunting one; dreams; transcriptions from relevant current reading; and occasionally—when it happens—perhaps the beginning of a poem. I also required that they "write up" each week's class, much as I myself had done for my Poetry Center students. This practice proved to be exceedingly useful to me, for in checking these over I was able to correct many misunderstandings of which I might never otherwise have become aware. They served, in fact, as a useful measure of my own clarity in explication, or lack of it.

The only poetry-writing assignment in this class consisted of work in translation; and it was interesting to me to discover that the level of writing was uniformly higher when the students were working from another language than it was when they were attempting to write original poems. I have since seen the same thing happen with other groups of students. The explanation is simple: students, especially young ones, unless quite exceptionally gifted, simply don't have the technical equipment to deal verbally with the tumult and confusion of their own thoughts and feelings. When they find a poem in another language (with or without a prose literal to help them understand it) that seems to speak for them or for which they feel some empathy, the relief at discovering the groundwork already done, the experience already in focus, the image emerged, releases untapped reserves of language in them so that even if their translation is quite free, quite a personal interpretation or adaptation of the original, it will usually show a competence, a craftsmanship, far in advance of their other writing.

We had the advantage of holding our three-hour sessions in a small secluded building. A kitchen adjoined the classroom, so that when we took our break we could make coffee. This helped the students feel there was something special, intimate, and exclusive about being in the poetry course (the first of its kind at Drew), which they enjoyed. However, I overestimated the degree to which this feeling of intimacy and of shared experience would extend through the rest of each week for them. Because it was a residential campus, and not a very large school, I assumed, in my ignorance of college life, that they would surely meet frequently in the course of their daily activities; but since they were of different academic years, and not all English majors, this was not true. Moreover, since poetry was of supreme importance to me I presumed it was so for them also and that they would therefore create opportunities to meet and talk about each other's work between classes; but in fact, while for a few writing was a major interest, for the majority it was quite naturally only one among several equal preoccupations. It was not until the tragic death of one member of this class the following summer that I realized how much less all of them had known about each other (except in the case of one or two close friendships that had existed before the class began) than I did about each one. I wrote a letter to the whole class and sent xeroxed copies to each member, thinking that this boy's death would have been the grief and shock to them that it was to me and that such a letter might be helpful and even necessary; but though their replies did express sorrow, it was for someone almost a stranger to all but one.

Retrospectively I felt that though most of these students worked hard, were interested, and showed definite, if varying, degrees of development in their work during the year—some, indeed, writing poems I thought extremely beautiful, and others "getting at things," making discoveries, in their notebook writing that were of undeniable value, yet if they had had the kind of extra-curricular interchanges—the hours over coffee, or late at night in someone's room, reading poems aloud, arguing, dreaming together—that I naively imagined were the heart of student life (as they are in books— old or European books, alas!) and would be especially prevalent among a bunch of hopeful poets—if they had had just this they might have gone much further in their understanding of poetry— further both as readers and writers. Even if we had met twice, instead of once, a week, it would have helped. Or if I had been living on campus instead of merely taking the train from New York just in time to eat lunch and go to class, returning directly after it was over (laden with papers which I began to read in the train—consumed, I may add, with the kind of curiosity about what the kids had produced this week that only a non-career, part-time teacher is prone to . . .).

C.C.N.Y. I

Meanwhile different things were happening for me at C.C.N.Y. Physically, to begin with, the setup could not have been more different. My trips to Drew included a delightful ferry ride and a train ride which—though I used to return home spent—I always found agreeable, much of it running between old backyards full of trees; and the Drew campus is spacious and green. My C.C.N.Y. class was scheduled early enough in the morning so that it was impossible to avoid the subway rushhour; then, always overloaded with books, a steep uphill walk through a housing project and a slum street to the old English building, where the elevator was usually out of order or hopelessly crowded and the corridors and stairs jammed with students milling about between classes. Save for the absence of shouting monitors and the size of the students, it was, in fact, almost indistinguishable from a typical New York elementary school. Arrived at the third floor, I would be caught— unless I arrived late—in the two-way traffic at the door of my classroom, where students issuing from a class taught there during the previous hour were trying to force their way out against the stream of my students trying to force their way in. The room was invariably strewn with cigarette butts, for though smoking was apparently not forbidden no ashtrays were provided. The room was dingy, the noise from outside—though we were on the "quiet" side of the building—often considerable. Only the students, with their hungry eyes, amazingly varied shapes and sizes, and equally varied styles of dress, were beautiful.

Yes, they were beautiful in their variety, their discontent, their hunger for life and poetry. But I missed the boat with them almost completely that first semester. I made several miscalculations, failed to get through to all but a few of them, and comparing them with my attentive and willing Drew students felt for the latter a love that these difficult and demanding big-city products did not— collectively—elicit from me.

My first miscalculation was in the number of students I accepted for the course. I no longer remember if it was suggested to me by the department that I take as many as possible, or whether I simply decided, since there was no orderly and rational way to choose among them anyway, to let them all come. But in any case, for the kind of course I had in mind to give, there was too large a number—between twenty-five and thirty. In a once-a-week course lasting, in this instance, only one semester, it is impossible for a non-resident teacher to get to know that many students in anything but a very superficial way. In fact, though I announced my availability after class each week for conferences (held in my cubicle-office across the hall), the schedules of many students made it impossible for them to come and see me.

My second miscalculation was in the nature of the course itself. I had been given carte blanche, indeed my invitation was basically to make myself available weekly as a representative "practicing poet," so that student poets would have the opportunity of association with a professional. Therefore—partly for a change, and because I felt that to teach two workshop courses concurrently would be at the very least confusing to me, and worse, monotonous; partly because it was obvious that the work of each individual in such a large group could not possibly be adequately discussed—I decided to make this a kind of lecture series, though they were to be very informal, interruptible lectures, leading, I hoped, to plenty of free discussion. My plan was to start from myself and work outward: to give a picture of one poet's—my own—early influences—beginning with nursery rhymes and Beatrix Potter—and formative experiences describing

what seemed to me my own beginnings as a poet; and going on to
my coming to America, the impact of American poetry on me, and
the interplay between me and some of my contemporaries. It was
not meant, of course, to be a mere autobiographical excursion; I
was to be only the starting point and the connecting thread; the
reading would not consist of my own poems (which, again naïvely,
I assumed that—once signed up for my course—they would read
from simple curiosity, if they had not, indeed, signed up precisely
because they *had* read them: both false assumptions), but of,
first, fairy tales and English poets, especially the thirties' poets
who were my first introduction to contemporary writing; then
Williams, Pound, Stevens, and on to Duncan and Creeley and
to poets younger than myself about whose work I was excited
that year—all the way, in fact, from my curiously Victorian childhood reading in England, the tail end of the 1930's caught hold of
through my older sister, the British "New Romantic" movement
of the forties, then the revelation of Williams, the development of
the so-called Black Mountain School, and right on into the advance guard of their own generation. I believed that peculiar as
my own life as a poet was, with my private education, mixed
(racial and religious) background, unusually early assumption
that I was a poet, and my having come to America only when I
was a year or two older than they now were—nevertheless it
would provide them, if they examined their own lives, with correspondences, equivalents. I wanted by dwelling upon my childhood to recall their own childhoods to them, as Rilke advised the
Young Poet to do; and thought that in searching out clues to their
own impulses to write, they might find unexpected sources of
strength. I wanted, by suggesting how erratic and fortuitous (and
nevertheless profitable) a poet's reading might have been, to
stimulate in them an exploratory spirit; and by announcing my
own lack of formal training, free them a little from the tyranny of
grades and course reading. I wanted, instead of anything re-
sembling a survey course on modern poetry, to give them as it
were an inside—though necessarily very partial—view of con-

temporary poetry, as for example, in what I would have told them of the interchanges of work and news and friendship that come to be called, by critics, a "school."

I still think it was a good idea—for a course given under certain circumstances, almost none of which were present in this case. I have thought in some detail about what these ideal circumstances would be, and shall list them: (1) A full year, not one semester, in which to give the course. (2) A small number of students—not exceeding sixteen, but not less than ten—because there should be (3) as much variety as possible in their personal backgrounds (the C.C.N.Y. class fulfilled this condition especially in comparison to Drew, as far as ethnic origins were concerned; but their economic and educational backgrounds were almost equally homogeneous). (4) They should all be of the same academic year (preferably juniors and seniors); should all have a fairly good knowledge of poetry up to, say, Yeats and Eliot; and should all have done *some* reading, however random, of contemporary American poetry. (5) They should all be at least as serious about writing poetry as students who enroll in a workshop, since the course would be at least partly an examination of what experiences, what kind of reading (and other art-experiences), what kind of living, seems conducive to writing. Or, from hearing about one poet's life at firsthand, what parallels can you draw from your own? (6) The physical circumstances in which the course is taught should be as intimate, comfortable, and generally conducive to relaxed discussion as possible (of course, I think this is a desirable condition for any class). My attempt to teach this course at C.C.N.Y. was a fiasco because none of these conditions were present, with the partial exception of #3 as noted.

On the contrary, there was hardly time to get started; there were too many students (few of whom knew each other before or became acquainted during the semester); and their educational background was in almost all cases New York City public schools, which is to say that they were culturally deprived. C.C.N.Y., with rather high standards and many devoted teachers, cannot with the best will in the world compensate in two, three, or four years for the shortcomings of bad grade and high schools. I must emphasize that an astonishingly high proportion of these students in my estimation (and probably according to IQ counts too) were brilliant. But almost all were grossly ignorant.

It is hard to describe this ignorance. There was a lot that they knew, academically—that is, they had taken certain courses and learned therefore the contents of those courses. But—this being a big university—few of them had taken the *same* courses, it seemed, and what they had not yet studied in a course they had no conception existed at all. If all had at least had the *same* lacunae!—but as it was, there was no common knowledge, nothing shared, no shared culture in fact—except that culture of the streets and playgrounds and comic books of their childhoods, which *I* could not penetrate because *I* had not shared them. I don't mean to give the impression that C.C.N.Y. students are illiterate, or not in any conventional use of the word. One girl in this class, I remember, gave a most beautiful, deeply felt, and thoroughly prepared talk on a difficult e. e. cummings poem; a young man, obviously headed for "Grad. School," discussed the prosody of—was it Spenser? Donne?—with devastating erudition (and perhaps a certain spite, because I had shown a disinclination to do anything of that kind); and another gifted and sensitive girl brought in a kind of homage-to-Williams poem that showed she had read Williams deeply and thoroughly—and not for a course, either. But it seemed as if each individual had a specialty and none had a common frame of reference, so that each allusion I made—and such a course as I was attempting, with its personal core and its wide range of citations, must of necessity depend largely on comprehensible, suggestive allusion—was picked up by only one or two students.

What these marvelous, interesting, challenging students had been deprived of was a sense of historical continuity, of context—the very thing a liberal education should provide. (And this was not the fault, most definitely, of C.C.N.Y.'s English department, but of a much larger situation—of all that is wrong with our society and especially with our cities.) It angers me when I think of it—and I also feel unhappy with myself for not having realized it sooner, so that I could have done more to redeem what for most of them must have been a wasted semester, as far as that class was concerned. What in fact happened was that I did not pursue my original plan very far, since while I did so they sat restless and—or so it seemed to me—either bored or angry. But I did not come up with a satisfactory substitute; instead I tried one thing and then another: one week a discussion of some contemporary poems (chosen usually by a student)—Creeley, Corso, e. e. cummings—a great favorite among them, incidentally, and not, in general, with me—Ginsberg, are those I remember—and the next, of some student's poems—discussions which failed, usually, to come to grips with anything, but slid off into purely subjective "likes" and "dislikes" because we had not established any evaluative standards; or conversations on life in general which almost said something but, again, fell short of their potential because we did not know each other well enough or because the bell would ring at the crucial moment—and which anyway did not involve enough of the people present.

Some time after the semester began there was some improvement brought about by the simple fact of our suddenly—myself and several other students—deciding to move the two long tables so that, instead of being end to end, with great distance between the people sitting at the two extremes, they were side by side so as to form a large square. This necessitated sudden physical activity for everyone in the room, as all the chairs had to be moved. A wonderful moment!—everyone in motion, talking, laughing, swearing, and a tremendous noise not just floating in irritatingly from somewhere else but made by us . . . With the exception of—alas—the last class of the semester, when too late a parallel sense of involvement and interchange seemed to occur, but on a less physical, more intellectual level, which might have led to good things if there had been a second semester to follow it up—this stands out for me as the most interesting experience of that fall, as far as the class as a group was concerned. There were, of course some individual good things that happened too, things said or written by one or another student that I found exciting, or things I said or did that a single student or a few found valuable; but little else that I think was shared by everyone.

Perhaps a group experience is less important in a class small enough for each individual member of it to receive—whether from teacher or fellow student—an *epiphany* at some time or other; but when a class is held once a week for only one semester and there are more than fifteen people enrolled in it, there is a mathematical likelihood that this kind of individual epiphany will occur only for a minority. Somehow, instead, I think the teacher must generate, and ferment among the students, enough passion and drama to produce a *collective* epiphany; and this not for its own sake (for it is hard to evaluate the depth or lasting value of such collective experiences) so much as for the sake of its function as gateway, portal, to new levels of feeling, to a greater openness after passing through it, and the sense of comradeship that can develop even among quite a large number of people who have been together in a time of crisis or revelation.

When I ask myself how I might have done better with those students in those three months, I come up with no satisfying answers. I could have put it up to them, right at the outset: what kind of class did they hope this would be? Let everyone make suggestions, and vote on them. But I was a total stranger to them, and they were, with—as I've said—a kind of typical big-city cageyness (the result of having had to develop strong defenses in the streets and schools just to survive), distrustful of strangers and therefore unlikely to have made many really sincere suggestions. When the course ended we had just come to the point, I believe, where they *could* have thrashed out among themselves and with me a plan for how to use a *second* semester.

Alternatively, I could have conducted a conventional lecture course on a selection of contemporary poets, with time for questions and discussion and with writing assignments each week. This would have been familiar to them and they would probably not have felt they were wasting their time. But again, many might, not unjustly, have felt disappointment at getting from a "visiting poet" merely *more of the same,* something a professional academic might have given them just as well or better.

C.C.N.Y. II

Though I considered the fall a fiasco, I was asked to teach at C.C.N.Y. for the spring term also, and accepted dubiously but in the hope of redeeming my failure even though with a new set of students. (I continued to see three or four members of the "fiasco" class occasionally, either in conference or—later—at meetings of this second group.) I limited enrollment, and devoted the first, and half of the second, session to getting acquainted, for I intended this to be more of a workshop and believed that freedom and honesty of discussion in a poetry workshop depended heavily on each member having some sense of the value of every other member.

This time I was blessed with students who were, I feel, even more responsive to this kind of situation than even the best of the first group might have been if the fall enrollment had been similarly limited. Though they shared the New York City public school background I have described, their defenses were not up even at the very beginning. I don't think this was due to my establishing, as far as I could, an ideal circumstance, but to some fortunate "psychological chemistry."

I began by asking each one to tell their name and something about their family background, and when and how they had first begun to write poetry (several had first done so through the encouragement or example of a single memorable and inspiring eighth- or ninth-grade teacher); expecting to have to coax this information from them. But on the contrary: launched into autobiography, it was hard to stop them—and they listened eagerly, as if hungry for just such information about each other. Indeed, as I came to realize, in the hurried, scattered life of a big non-residential university it is quite possible for a student to go from class to class all year without knowing much more of his fellow students than he knows of the people whom he sees each day in the subway (and such is the routine of many lives that the same people do actually sit—or stand—in the same car of the same train day after day on their way to job or school. But only an emergency, such as the blackout that struck the East a couple of years ago, breaks down their mutual reserve).

We found that our group included a Puerto Rican boy who was a painter as well as a poet; a Chinese girl born in Hong Kong; a black girl who was a blues and folk singer and had been to Africa the year before in connection with some intercultural project; a Polish boy who had come to the U.S. when he was about seven years old and could still remember his farm home in Poland; a Jewish boy from the Bronx who was a twin—his twin brother and an older brother both wrote poetry also, it turned out; and so on, round the table—an extraordinarily interesting and varied ten or twelve kids (I am unsure, now, about the number, because a few members of the fall class joined this one on an informal basis). This was almost an ideal group for anyone to work with. Their talent and level of achievement varied, but all had a genuine and keen interest in poetry and were not just taking the course for an easy credit. We had from the beginning a genuinely friendly and even excited relationship. There was no one who really held back —even though, of course, some were more reserved or shy than others—and they actually did begin to do what I hoped for at Drew but which, even though it would have seemed easier to do at Drew, seemed rarely to happen there: they met after or between classes, in the cafeteria or elsewhere, and went on talking about each other's poems and about poetry and life in general.

As often as possible I invited them all to my apartment in downtown New York instead of holding an ordinary session in the noisy, ugly classroom; and though—because these living-room sessions had to be held in the evening, since in the daytime they had full schedules and, in some cases, part-time jobs as well—it was not possible to do this often, yet the intimacy and social familiarity these few occasions gave were a definite help in increasing the cohesiveness and interaction that came to exist among them. I don't imply that all of them met together out of class; but a few had known one another before, and certain others became close friends during the semester; so that most of them gathered in groups of from two or three to five and six. At the end of the year I suggested that they try to remain in touch during the summer, so that in the fall we could continue to meet at my house whenever I could manage it; and a number of them did this. The next winter, though circumstances prevented my doing this on a regular once-a-month basis, we did gather perhaps five times at my apartment, and what was even better, they met a number of times at each other's homes. The learning from each other which took place then—and for a few of them still continues today—as seen in the work several continue to send me from time to time, is one of the greatest pleasures I have known in my teaching experience so far.

Until almost the end of the year I was quite cautious about letting occasional auditors into the classroom for fear of disturbing our sense of privacy. (I consulted them about this and they agreed.) But toward the end I did let a few congenial extra students in occasionally; and to the meetings we held in my apartment the following fall and winter I sometimes invited other young—and sometimes older—poets, especially my former Poetry Center students, two or three of whom were by then editing a magazine to which, eventually, some of the C.C.N.Y. students contributed (one, in fact, has since become one of the editors), and a few from Drew, and now and again (it would have been oftener but for the distance) some of my Vassar students—for by then I was teaching at Vassar. On these occasions what occurred was not so much a class as an open poetry reading; the room was crowded to bursting, thick with smoke, and littered cheerfully with wine glasses and coffee cups. The value of so gathering—aside from the fact that it was fun—was that it gave young writers an opportunity to be heard by, and to hear, a larger group of their peers than the small class afforded, and—bound as we were by a shared passion for poetry—to feel some sense of there being (as I believe there is, despite all people will say about professional backbiting and intrigue) a community of poets, a sense of belonging to a Mystery, a guild. Criticism would be offered from fresh sources; the way a poem sounded in a larger context, a context of listeners not all of whom knew what development had taken place in the writer's work in the past six months was often a revelation; and sometimes a particularly warm response—applause even—would give pleasure and new confidence to a kid that needed it. My function became more and more that of a hostess and occasional point of reference; they were not dependent on me.

But I have run ahead of myself. What actually went on during the spring semester classes at City College, and what of that cultural deprivation of which I spoke in describing my initial impressions there? Well, that existed among this group too; but somehow, among such a small number it didn't seem to get in the way. Because they got to know each other so much better than the average class, and were so varied in background and knowledge, each contributed something which all the others seemed to pick up on, and so individual deficiencies were to a large extent compensated for: I think that is the explanation. As to what we did: basically the course was not very different from those at the Poetry Center and at Drew—an attempt to supply, by discussion of technical elements and of "stance" (i.e., the emotional, moral, and aesthetic attitudes of the artist), some underpinnings for judgment or—a better word —evaluation of their own work; an emphasis on *listening to the sounds* of poetry, not reading merely with the eye, and upon experiencing the poem as a sonic entity before embarking on any analysis of its parts; and concomitantly, upon learning—as a part of one's responsibility to the art one serves—to read aloud slowly and clearly.

Here too, as at Drew and later at Vassar, I tried to get them to develop a sense of the concrete and particular instead of writing about their "feelings" in vague abstract terms. This emphasis had been less necessary at the Poetry Center, where the class members were mostly older and more developed as poets. It is, however, almost always essential with younger students, as I have found not only with those I have taught on a regular basis but also from the many occasional seminars I have conducted when visiting colleges for a few days at a time and from the poems and letters often sent to me by unknown student readers (many of whom seem, in innocent egotism, to look on any published poet as an on-tap Free University-by-mail!). I shall return to this question of the concrete and sensuous in more detail when I come to speak of my Vassar class.

Notebooks were again emphasized as important tools for their development (but not, in this case, examined by me unless at the request of an individual), and assignments were very few and consisted, I think, exclusively of reading and of translation. I read aloud to them a good deal, and it was I think with this class that I first tried out Muriel Rukeyser's wonderful idea of having a whole class read a poem one after another, without previous discussion— something which perhaps sounds boring but in fact turns out to be a sort of alchemical process, a process of filtering, refining, and intensification of understanding that is far more effective and moving than any mere analytical method can be. Usually the first one or two readers stumble and hesitate; the next two read with some confidence and facility; then a period of boredom and irritation may set in—probably most participants feeling they can't bear to hear those same words one more time; and then—subtly—that point is passed, and one finds oneself at a different level of response, finds oneself emerging into an intimate, sensuous comprehension of the poem that activates both intellect and imagination. I have never known it to fail (though I have not discovered what the optimum number of participants is for this technique—too few, obviously, would in this case probably be worse than too many).

It was not innovations or inventiveness on my part, then, that made this class in most ways the best I have yet experienced, but the fact that I, as well as the students, was relaxed, encouraged, and confident. For the first time I found myself sitting back and letting them do the talking. At the Poetry Center I had sometimes turned the class over to one of the members for some special topic —syllabics, or new methods of measuring quantity (in reference to

Williams' "variable foot")—of which their knowledge was obviously
greater than mine; and at Drew I asked students, on occasion, to
prepare and deliver a talk on some writer in whom they were especially interested. But with this group I was able to let discussion
ramble without tensely feeling I was no longer in charge and that
if I were not in charge they would feel cheated, ultimately, and
not give me their attention when I wanted it. On the contrary, I was
now able to rejoice in their being in charge of themselves; and of
course, concomitantly, their trust in me, and respect for me, was
much greater, I believe, than that of students with whom I was
more authoritarian. With them, incidentally, I became in the most
natural way Denise, instead of Miss Levertov. Even with the Poetry
Center class, though as I have said they were mainly quite accomplished poets, and older than average too, I remained Miss Levertov
in the classroom till the end of the course; and at Drew there
seemed no inclination to address me less formally, and indeed I
think I would have embarrassed those students by indicating that I
didn't care what they called me. Yet *I* always addressed everyone
by their first name without even thinking about it—even at Vassar
where there is an old-fashioned habit of calling the girls Miss This
and Miss That, upheld I suppose by male teachers who want to
maintain a convenient sense of distance from an all-girl class.

I don't mean to suggest that all was perfect and everybody satis-
fied. We did have only one semester to work in, and so much to say
and do—and at the end of the year I was left with a sad feeling of
how much had been left out, how much confusion they still felt
among all the possibilities of the craft, how little they still knew of
their own possibilities. And the free meetings of the following
school year were not as frequent by any means as I had wished.
Nevertheless, it was an experience that remains for me a model of
how a poetry workshop can be at least the beginning of a kind of
community; and proof of how, for the "teaching" of poetry at least
—I have of course no knowledge of whether this would be true for
other studies—a community, an atmosphere of sharing which ex-
tends beyond the "subject" in hand, is the most conducive to real
learning, a learning in which the teacher shares.

Vassar I (Workshop)

At Vassar, the physical environment was all one could ask for. At the beginning and end of the year, at least, we held some classes outdoors in the parklike campus; and the classroom allotted to me was clean, quiet, and quite comfortable—though, since it had a long table it was not possible to move, and because smoking was not allowed, we eventually moved out to a social room in one of the dormitories where there were soft chairs, a rug, and people could sprawl or smoke if they wished. And the girls—thirteen to start with, then eleven, one leaving college for medical reasons and one leaving the class because she had decided she did not want to write poetry after all (she came back at the end of the year, informally)—had the kind of educational background C.C.N.Y. students generally lack. A surprising number of them were very definitely talented—to the degree that one could reasonably expect they might continue writing, and well, after they had left college. (There is, of course, a certain amount of creativity that seems a part of being young—not that it is to be despised. Or perhaps it is rather that the creative impulse in some individuals turns toward poetry at a certain period of their lives, though they are not definitively and inescapably poets and will later find their destiny elsewhere. But among these girls were several who perhaps would remain engaged with the art and find in it the focus of their lives, or so it seemed to me—and I shall only find out if I was right ten or twenty years from now.)

On the other hand, the fact that they were all girls and all sophomores and juniors was a disadvantage. The value of such a class being coed seems to lie not in the fact that more different points of view will be voiced (for ten girls are surely liable to have ten points of view as different from each other, taking into account similarity of age and social background, as five boys and five girls) but in the tendency of boys to be more outspoken, less dominated by the desire to please or fear of committing themselves, which, consciously or unconsciously, seems to affect a group of girls unleavened by a masculine element. (I arrived at this supposition from talking to the girls themselves about the problem. A number of them said that in coed high school classes they had been less afraid to venture opinions.) It is not that boys talk more than girls, but when they do talk they are more apt to blurt out their true feelings. So for a good part of the first term we moved cagily—I trying to get them to talk more freely, and especially to talk *to each other* and not address all their remarks to me; and they resisting, and mistrustful of each other, almost as my first C.C.N.Y. students had been mistrustful of *me*.*

By the Christmas vacation I was depressed and so were they; it seemed as if despite talent and excellent conditions, and despite all I felt I had learned at C.C.N.Y. the previous spring, this class was not going to be a success. But somehow after the vacation and the exam period was over (there were no exams in this course but they had naturally been affected by the tension and anxiety of those in their other subjects) a change seemed to occur for no discernible reason—unless it was the departure of the two girls who dropped the course, though neither had been a disruptive element. Those who remained seemed to draw closer together; something had crystallized, settled. They were now less eager for tête-à-têtes with me, more willing to share ideas and responses with each other. And by the end of the year the level of constructive, appreciative, and intelligent response they were exchanging was in gratifying contrast to the "Like–Don't like" style in which they had begun their association.

My principle efforts with this group were to shake them loose a bit from their timid perfectionism—probably an endemic trouble in the more conservative women's colleges, with high entrance requirements and consequently a high proportion of nervously ambitious girls, the former academic stars of their secondary schools— and to awaken their powers of sensuous observation (often neglected since early childhood in favor of a one-sided intellectuality), as the only foundation for technical development in the art

* This is curiously different from what I've since learned in Women's Liberation groups.

of poetry. So few of them, gifted though they were, seemed ever to have really looked at anything. They walked through that beautiful park with their heads down and their thoughts anywhere but on the natural world. It was not that I wanted them to write "about" Nature—but in fact they were living among, for instance, some of the finest trees I have ever seen, and I thought it as essential for them to notice the fact as I would for a city dweller to notice, say, the movement of people on the streets or the reflection of traffic lights on wet pavement at night.

To demonstrate the principle of what I would call the *unsought* objective correlative I brought in some fallen leaves, one for each student, and asked them to write objectively on what they saw. As some sort of model, I had first read them some of Francis Ponge's prose poems, which are phenomenological descriptions of the utmost freshness; as well as some quotations from Rilke's letters, about *looking*, about the kind of humble yet passionate looking that woos a Thing to reveal itself, and which proves to reveal also far more about individual feeling and "voice" than any introspective abstraction. This first in-class assignment produced a general level of writing much higher than most of what they had been doing on their own, and they did not fail to recognize it. The reason was similar to that I have suggested earlier as the reason students write better when they are translating than when dealing directly with their own content; but in this case it was not so much that they were not "starting from scratch" as that they were discovering how the filters of the senses (in this instance, sight, and to a lesser extent, touch) don't subvert but intensify the action on language of underlying mood or preoccupation. Or to put it another way, that there is no purely objective and no purely subjective art—the objective is necessary to genuine "expression," and subjective "feeling" to genuine objectivity. Translating, again—with all its varied technical possibilities—is a marvelous exercise, but I emphasized that it would only be really fruitful if they chose originals for which they felt some affinity.

Other assignments included taking a poem of their own and turning it into plain prose: which revealed the weakness of bad poems and the strengths of good ones; and free-associating (this was a limbering-up exercise) on themes I gave them. The words allotted—which included Fear, Anger, Discovery, Birth, Entrance, among others—had been carefully chosen for each individual as highly emotive for her, my choice being based on what I had by then learned of her both in class and in conference and from her work. I had not, on principle, asked them to write poems—just to write; but as it turned out, many of them did write poems in the course of this and other in-class assignments, or later developed notes written in class time into poems; and in some cases—for reasons I don't understand—these were some of the best work they did all year.

This fact caused me to relax somewhat, as the year went on, my stringency in regard to assigning any poem writing. I was still— and I am sure will remain—cautious about the value of external pressure on the creative impulse, for I detest the clever verse disguised as poetry that emanates so frequently from the academic poetry factories and makes its way so efficiently in the world, acclaimed by reviewers who, like the verse writers, suppose poetry to be a way of *manipulating* language. But I did begin to suggest that, if they were brewing a poem anyway, they should consider whether this particular material—or some notebook material they had not yet developed—might not lend itself to a narrative form, for instance, or to the form of a dialogue, instead of taking for granted that, because they had done "lyrics" before, it would have the form of a short lyric. One of our most frequent topics of discussion all along was the relation of form to content, not only in the basic word-to-word and line-to-line sense in which one must discuss any poem under close scrutiny, but in the larger sense of what, in the intrinsic nature of content, makes one poem seed grow into a dramatic monologue and another into a ballad, or a sonnet, or a song.

Since it was too far for these students conveniently to come down to New York to participate in those poetry parties I used to enjoy with the C.C.N.Y. group and other young poets, I decided to start Open Readings at Vassar when, in the spring, I moved up there to live for the ten weeks my husband was at Stanford teaching in the Voice Project.* We made posters and invited anyone to come who was writing poetry, to read or just to listen. There were many girls who were not in my class, or in any class where poems were read, but who were writing poetry; and though not all my own students came to the Open Readings regularly or at all, those who did found these new associates stimulating; while the unknown poets themselves, appearing out of the woodwork, rejoiced in discovering a kind of non-credit class and—again—some sense, I think, of community. A few faculty came to these sessions also; one of whom disturbed me by trying, I felt, to over-formalize them by his too-dogmatic comments and by not waiting to be *asked* to comment. His intentions were kind; but my idea was that Open Readings should have a very free atmosphere and not merely be extra classes, though criticism would be available for those who desired it; and that critical comment should not come exclusively from me or from any other faculty member, but should be a matter of peer response. I tried to emphasize this by reading work-in-progress of my own and getting other faculty to do so—in fact, I tried as far as possible to ensure that no one who was not prepared to throw his or her own work into the arena with everyone else's should offer criticism (though, of course, anyone could come as a listener)—and to reduce my own function to seeing that all who wished got a chance to read and were not swamped by the more aggressive.

Some boyfriends and students from a nearby men's college came to one or two of the Open Readings, which was a pleasure after our segregated classes. And some foreign students read in their own languages, which gave us an interesting chance to listen to sounds we did not understand (Israeli and, as I recall, Pakistani) which yet we could hear were the sounds of poetry. It was interesting too to note that, while some of the poetry being written "on their own" by girls who had never been in a "workshop" was every bit as

---

* I am not here describing the Voice Project (initiated by John Hawkes and funded by the Office of Education for, alas, only a single year), since it will be documented elsewhere in this volume, representing as it does the most intensive use of writers as teachers yet undertaken anywhere.

good as some of that being written under a poet's guidance, the quality of evaluative, constructive criticism my students were by that late spring able to offer was much higher. They could see why and how a poem was or was not an achieved work, where even accomplished writers who had not done the kind of thinking about craft that they had done were unable to express distinctions or put their finger on what was wrong. This gave me great pleasure, for I felt I had in some substantial measure achieved one of my principal goals: to put underpinnings of understanding beneath "talent." It has been said that talent is of no use without character. I don't know if I agree—it depends on what is meant by character. But I do know talent is effervescent and easily corrupted without a sense of responsibility to craft, of art as a power to which talent may be dedicated *and which demands of its votaries something more than to be used by them for the relief of moods.*

The other principal success in this class was the way the students came during the year to have more tolerance and even respect for each other—even for the less talented among their number. This was partly due to the fact that even the two or three who perhaps should not have been in the class in the first place, because they were neither as capable nor as concerned as the rest, did make some progress either in their writing or their insights as readers, or both; and partly because, since I made a point of taking everybody seriously, assuming they were doing the best they could, the more arrogant members gradually began to do so too.

I think what *I* learned from *them* that year was also more tolerance: I came to see more clearly how precarious the confidence of the seemingly confident young really is, how a piece of writing that to me might seem—seen objectively—weak and banal may mean much to them as a step along their own road; so that though one does not want to let them think they have done something marvelous when they haven't, though one wants to make them learn to make demands on their own capacities and not be self-satisfied, yet it is even more important not to discourage them, by an unfeeling excess of candor, from taking the *next* step. The situation is different with older writers in a student relationship:

the middle-aged who have only just begun to write, or who have been writing for years and still write badly, are, I think, extremely unlikely to develop further and it is kinder to let them know it, in most cases.

Vassar II

This was a concurrent class of another kind: a senior seminar in modern poetry, the first and, so far, the only non-workshop class I have taught. We read Yeats, Pound, Eliot, Williams, Stevens, H. D., Lawrence, Creeley, and Duncan. If it differed from other such seminars in being taught by a poet, not scholar, it was perhaps chiefly in that, with the exception of Eliot, all the poets studied were of great importance to me as a *writer,* not only as a reader. Talking about a poet who has been or continues to be a personal influence is inevitably, even if subtly, different from talking about a writer to whom one stands, however admiringly or pleasurably, only in the relation of reader.

It was an exciting class to teach, not only because I enjoyed the close reading and thinking it made necessary, but because, through the many excellent papers the students wrote, and in the course of sometimes quite heated discussions, I made so many discoveries and rediscoveries. Not all were English majors—four or five out of the ten—but all had had exactly that kind of civilizing, connective education I had missed in my first C.C.N.Y. class: one could—with occasional exceptions—make allusions without drawing blanks, and if an individual did not know about something one assumed she did know, the tendency was for her to go off and look it up without being urged to do so.

Vassar's English department in general discourages the use of secondary sources, so my emphasis on reading not what critics had said but rather the respective poets' own prose writings—essays, autobiographies, letters, and so on—as adjuncts to the reading of the poems themselves, was not an innovation. Having the students keep, for a period of some weeks, Poetry Reading Journals, was however, something new, and proved enjoyable to them and important to me for the insights they gave me both into the readers' individual approaches and, often through them, into the poems read. These notebooks took the place of regular papers for a while, and were intended to be regular annotations upon their current reading in poetry, not necessarily confined to the poets we were studying in class. They could be as informal as anyone wanted; I hoped they would reveal some interplay between our studies and their free reading, and between their daily lives and other studies and their awareness of poetry. And this did in fact happen. Some girls, indeed, continued to keep the journals going after the assignment was over and we had returned to more formal papers. However, even such papers were not required to be as formal as in most of their courses (or so they seemed to feel)—that is to say, while I expected them to do the required reading conscientiously (which was no problem, as they were really interested) I did not have the scholar's horror of the impressionistic paper, if it was well written, and I encouraged them to forget the boring impersonality many had learned was the proper approach (in preparation, alas, for Grad. School!) and try to get hold of their genuine reactions instead of trying to feel what they thought they ought to feel. I find nothing more tiresome than reading papers written in the tone of patronizing omniscience common to many academic critics. What is wrong with saying flatly "I think," "My reaction was"? But even in high school so many good students are browbeaten into thinking it is insolent or in bad taste to use the personal pronoun in an assigned paper.

My great hope in this course was to confirm those who were already readers of poetry in their love for it, and awaken that love in those who were in the course because it was their last chance, before graduation, to find out a bit about the subject. I was not out to prepare anyone for graduate school or help make scholars. Those who were going to be scholars were already excellently prepared by their four years at a college which gives the best academic training I have yet encountered. What I wanted was to make good readers of them, so that their reading would be an enduring resource to them no matter what they were going to do after graduation. As in poetry-writing courses, I emphasized the sonic, and to this end—as well as reading aloud to them and getting them to read—made frequent use of tapes and records. More often than in workshop classes our discussion led to consideration of ideas and attitudes. They didn't talk as much as I would have wanted, but their enthusiasm can be judged from their having attended voluntarily an extra class I gave in Study Week and from the fact that several wrote on their final exam that the exam itself had been a pleasure. As for myself, I felt privileged to have spent a reading year with such agreeable and enlivening companions.

Influences

I began to teach with nothing but an anxious desire to share as much as I could of what I had learned in a life spent since childhood in engagement with poetry. Though skeptical of the need for anyone who was really likely to be a poet to attend such a class at all, I wanted to make it as useful as possible since these people had in fact elected to do so. I wanted to give them ground rules, and pack enough into one course to cause them to desist from shopping around for further courses of the same type: there is something sad in the veteran of many workshops who is still not a poet and never will be. I wanted to teach the kind of course that would reveal to the *non*-poet that he was on the wrong track, and define more clearly for the *possible* poet what his own voice was. But I had done little if any thinking about how much the possibility of imparting anything might depend on the degree of authoritarianism or permissiveness of the teacher. In occasional seminars and in giving free criticism to various young poets, I had not had to face this problem. My attitude tends naturally to be rather friendly, informal, and respectful of the individual's effort (unless I take a capricious dislike to him, which is not frequent) and it was not until I taught a regular course that I discovered how authoritarian

I could be under pressure of my uncertainty of my own ability to satisfy expectations in a new role, and at the same time the conviction that I knew things they didn't know—knowledge which I was eager to give them. However, at about the same time that I became conscious of how tightly I was keeping the reins in my hands I was fortunately exposed, at the series of conferences of teachers and writers held in several locations in the New York area in 1965–66, to the ideas and educational hopes of people more experienced than myself, and whose concern was more directly with *how* to teach and *how* to learn than mine (whose deepest allegiance was to poetry itself, not to teaching).

Chief, I think, among these influences, was Sam Moon, of Knox College, Illinois, brought to the Writers and Teachers conferences through my husband, who had spent a week at Knox and been much impressed with his journal of a teaching experiment, "Teaching the Self" (subsequently published in *Improving College & University Teaching*, Autumn, 1966, Vol. XIV, #4). I had long since read some A. S. Neill, also Caroline Pratt's *I Learn from Children*; both deal with childhood education that provides tools, information, and the freedom to use them and trusts children will have the curiosity and care to utilize what is so provided, when the teacher is guide, philosopher, and friend, but not a dogmatic authority; and I believed them. But I had not thought much about how to put the same principles into action with college students, nor how to adapt non-authoritarian practice to my own temperament, or my temperament to it. Sam Moon's experiment, the account Florence Howe and Paul Lauter gave of their work with a Summer Institute of high school teachers and students (who lived for several weeks on an absolutely equal basis, both in and out of classes) and the temperamental ability, as a teacher, of my husband, Mitch Goodman, to refrain from dominating his students—the confidence in himself and in them that made it possible for him to endure silences in his classes, at times, of a kind I had always nervously filled up—these were among the factors that began to have an effect on my attitude to my responsibilities and opportunities as a teacher: though whatever change took place in me was not radical or dramatic and probably was not even noticeable to my students as a change.

I did not, and still do not, feel ready to attempt anything quite as decentralized as Sam Moon undertook—and indeed, I share the doubts he himself expresses in his concluding remarks on "Teaching the Self," concerning the degree of self-effacement desirable: the teacher's rights should surely be neither greater nor lesser than those of his students, but equal to theirs. One should control one's vivacity and loquacity only so far as is necessary to give the students a fair chance to bring forth theirs, but not so much as to deny one's own spontaneity and passion, nor to deny them its stimulus. But the philosophic basis of Moon's work, his modesty and honesty, and the evidence given in his students' comments on his experiment of their appreciation of his stance and of its value in their development will, I believe, continue to act for me as guides for my own future practice.

The student revolution, from Berkeley on, was not really an influence on me during the teaching experiences I have recounted, because at none of these colleges was it, during that period, an active force. There was at Vassar a small SDS group which was trying to promote curriculum reforms, but I felt so strongly that they were making a storm in a teapot and that their energies should, instead, have been directed to creating a strong anti-war movement in the college (something which did, that year, begin to form, but entirely without their help), that I took no interest in their activities —especially since, compared at any rate with what they would have had to put up with in the huge universities, it seemed to me that they had a minimum of justifiable academic grievances. It has been through my work with the growth of a Peace Council at Vassar and, in this past year,* when I have not been teaching but have toured the country visiting many campuses not only to read and talk about poetry but to speak about Draft Resistance and meet with Resistance groups, that I have come into direct and stimulating contact

* 1968.

with student power in action and learned to see how curriculum changes will and must arise naturally out of the greater maturity and self-dependence of a generation that has, in its best representatives, found the will to buck the Power Elite and to refuse to regard obedience as a virtue in itself: and in so doing has begun to discover hitherto unrealized possibilities of inner change and community.

Some Conclusions

1. I have been extremely fortunate in having been given, at each place I have taught, without exception, a completely free hand both as to what I taught and how I taught it and in the selection of students. This good fortune has, it is true, deprived me of the chance to contrast such conditions with more conventional ones; however, my husband, during the same period, had more varied conditions of teaching, ranging from large classes and a prescribed curriculum at Hofstra College and the C.C.N.Y. evening division to circumstances at Drew (where he taught the year after I did) identical with those I have described there, and to the Voice Project at Stanford where, to an even greater degree, every condition of freedom and autonomy was met. And his very strong sense of being able best to give and to receive in a small, seminar-type class where the materials used were chosen by himself and the students and not prescribed impersonally confirms my conviction that intimacy and flexibility are prerequisites to a good teaching-learning relationship. Lectures, surely, can only be adjuncts to the seminar—not vice versa.

2. Physically, a pleasant room in which smokers can smoke and lollers can loll seems quite important. If one is going to sit at a table, a round table would be preferable to the usual long rectangle. A noisy room, where one is continually interrupted by sounds of traffic or by talk from the corridor, is obviously distracting—but how little thought architects and planners seem to give to this rudimentary problem! Worst of all, in this connection, is the bell—the nerve-shattering, primitive device that plays Person from

Porlock with so many moments of revelation. If possible, poetry classes should be open-ended—i.e., scheduled at a time of day when no one has other classes immediately afterward.

3. The better students get to know each other out of class, the better they will use their time in class, and the better—thereby—the teacher will learn to listen to them and curb his tendency to boss them.

4. If the writer as teacher has a special contribution to make, it can only be, surely, his passion for his art and the story of his personal experience in his craft. Therefore he must put these unequivocally at the service of his students and not try to compete with the scholars or to protect himself by withholding his peculiarities. If he feels a need for such self-protection, he shouldn't be teaching at all. On the other hand, there is no denial, it seems to me, that teaching, even at its most rewarding, uses up some of the same kind of energies that go into his own work; therefore I think it is extremely risky for any artist to teach full-time—perhaps especially if he enjoys teaching. That very enjoyment can be a form of seduction, away from his own work—and so, ultimately, a bitterness. He is also more valuable to his students as a part-time or occasional teacher, because he is then ensured against staleness and the development of professional pedagogic tricks and brings to the class some of the excitement of having come freshly from the making of literature, rather than the study of what others have made. At the same time, I think it important not to *impose* on others the particularities of one's own point of view and one's own style. I bent over backward not to do this, and have taken pride in the fact that my writing students were not turning out imitations of my own poems. But in retrospect I think it might have been better to take more of a risk in that respect for the sake of sharing with them more of my current working experience, if I could have found a way to do so without violating my necessary solitude. This is a problem to be worked out, perhaps, in the future.

5. As to papers, other assignments, and grades: when, in Vassar II, I assigned papers, I proposed a subject but at the same time made it clear that if an individual found it more appropriate to

write about some other aspect of the poet we were studying she was free to do so. I wanted relevance, but I wanted independence also, and not to hear my own words parroted back to me. And I tried, in correcting papers, to stress the importance of good writing, both for its own sake and because the effort to write well promotes clearer thinking and more sensitive reading. Three of the last and best papers in this course were, respectively, a poem, a letter addressed to one of the poets we had read, and an account of the phases of response undergone by the writer in studying Robert Duncan's work and then hearing him read.

I have noted already that I came to modify my resistance to giving "creative" writing assignments to the extent of asking students to undertake the verbal equivalent of still-life drawings, or of attempting to free-associate as an equivalent of a dancer's stretching exercises. But I would still never demand a poem by a certain date or that it be written in a prescribed form.

I was obliged to give half-term and final grades in most of these courses, but made it clear at the start that no one would fail unless he had a grossly inadequate attendance record or had made no contribution at all. I gave (in the workshop courses) A's to those who had been writing exceptionally good poems and had also participated generously and usefully in discussion; B's to those who had written a few good poems, showed definite signs of development, and participated well in discussion; and a few C's to those who were neither productive nor spoke much in class. It so happened that at Vassar, at any rate—I no longer remember for sure whether this was so elsewhere—no one who was very active in discussion was notably unproductive of good poems. One girl rarely said a word in class but did write some good poems and was obviously serious about her work. She got a B. I would prefer a no-grading or pass-fail system, but as long as the whole spirit of a course ensures that people are not just working for grades but out of interest in the subject, I don't think it matters very much. In the Vassar senior seminar I tried to get them to adopt Sam Moon's plan, asking each student to suggest what she felt her final grade ought to be, but it didn't work out: some of the best students were too modest—and all of them hated the idea. Indeed, it seems feasible to me only in entirely student-run courses. I am not sure how such courses have been arranged in the Free Universities, but my idea of such a course would be that all the planning assignments and grading would be done by a student committee, or if possible by a whole-class voting system, with the "expert"—whether scholar or writer—called in to "do his stuff," but not to pass judgment on the students' achievement at all. Several such experts might be utilized in the semester. This might be a very fruitful way of study in a reading course, and would be a good way for the teaching writer, at any rate, both to avoid developing an autocratic mentality and expending his time and energy in correcting papers and so on, except in response to occasional requests. I don't think, however, that it would be suited to a workshop course, where students, especially beginners, need above all to gain some sense of initiation into the service and practice of an art, and some standards of evaluation, which they are not equipped to give each other but must be handed down by an older practitioner.

A Berkeley Postscript

I taught at Berkeley from January till early June of 1969—two quarters. Groovy Berkeley! My experiences there, brief though they were, make much of what I have written up to this point seem to me quaint and old-fashioned: My Berkeley students (in the classes called 143 and 108—the freshmen were another matter) demanded and gave more than any others I had known, and by their attitudes made me much more deeply and genuinely non-authoritarian. I grew younger there, and more open to suggestion; and at the same time more confident. There was no need of establishing and maintaining authority since I had their trust and they had mine. I could see that they respected me more for making and admitting mistakes than if I had carefully avoided any but "successful" sessions.

To be accurate, I met with two distinct adventures at the Uni-

versity of California. One was my first attempt to wrestle with an
ordinary, non-elite freshman class in Reading and Expository
Writing. The other was a brief but intense taste of the possibility
of true human community. I shall treat of them accordingly in
two sections, describing first the less satisfying, but nonetheless
valuable, segment of my Berkeley experience:

1. In English 1A, section something, I had the privilege of choosing
my own texts, but no choice of students. There were thirty of them,
preponderantly square, rather timid, and in a few cases semi-
illiterate kids; several were athletes, several (including one of the
most imaginative and sensitive) belonged to fraternities; quite a
large proportion of them were commuters (living with their
parents) and just about all of them were desperately worried about
grades. Why they were so different from the other two groups I
taught I was never sure. Did they represent a changing admissions
policy? Apparently not, since, supposedly, U. of California admissions are administered by computer (though this fact—the
standard answer to questions about possible changes in admissions
standards to favor "obedient," non-radical entrants—does not seem
to me to preclude the possibility of attitudes being fed into the
computer which, based on the applicants' social and "behavior"
records in high school, would tend to exclude the brilliant but
dissident). Had the remarkable, highly differentiated, third- and
fourth-year students in my other classes been as unawakened and
timid in their freshman year? Or was it simply that the kind of
student who applies for electives in poetry—writing and reading—
is such a special type of student that I had in fact never before
encountered anything but an elite? At all events, I found this class
pretty hard going, even though I had an excellent TA (the poet
David Bromige).

However, the principal event of the quarter was the Third World
Strike, which, while it made things more difficult for me in some
ways, probably brought the class further, if raising of consciousness
were the measure, than it could have gone in such a limited time
without it. I was in agreement with the principles of the strike,

even though I had many questions about its timing and tactics; so, when it was declared, I immediately announced my support of it to my class, and told them all my classes would be conducted off campus as long as it continued. There was no question in my mind about continuing to teach: in the three weeks or so that had passed before the strike began I had learned enough about these students to feel confident that I would serve the interests of the Movement and of the Third World infinitely better by staying with these kids and providing a forum for discussion of what was happening than by, as it were, abandoning them. Almost none of them were striking, and almost none of their other classes were taken off campus—the few that were were not conducted off campus in support of the strike but merely because some teachers feared violence and disruption. As far as I could gather, very little discussion of the issues took place either in these classes or in those that continued to be taught in the classrooms. Yet these students daily had to pass picket lines whose purpose they barely understood, and were witnesses to scenes of police brutality and to the reaction to it, without, I felt, receiving any help in interpreting these events unless I gave it.[*]

For the first few classes after we abandoned the classroom I could not find a suitable location: we met in a student's apartment in Oakland, which meant extra carfares and other inconveniences. There was some resentment, and a good deal of anxiety about the effect of this disruption on their (damned!) grades. One student (who later made his peace with me) complained to the Department Chairman. Many students were absent—not because they were striking, but because of the journey to and from Oakland. I began to feel the group, so tenuously established *as* a group in any real sense, was breaking hopelessly apart. But I then secured the hospitality of an excellent room in the Newman Center (Catholic Campus Ministry) near the campus, and things picked up again. Anxiety lessened, and they began—albeit grudgingly at first—to

---

[*] There were, of course, some other faculty members whose position was similar to mine; but I am speaking of the other classes in which these particular thirty students happened to be enrolled.

acknowledge the actual advantages of a more attractive and re-laxed setting, with comfortable chairs and a seminar atmosphere, which freshmen in a huge university so rarely experience.

Since the books I had chosen (providentially) for the course—*The Harmless People* by Elizabeth Marshall Thomas, *Etruscan Places* by D. H. Lawrence, *Division Street: America* by Studs Terkel, and *Night Flight to Hanoi* by Father Daniel Berrigan—all dealt with kinds of human community (or, in the case of *Division Street*, with its absence too), it was not difficult to coordinate discussion of strike issues, and the broader ones of war, violence, and institutionalized injustice, with the reading material. When they experienced their first tear-gassing and, though they were not strikers but just happened to be in the Plaza at the time, found themselves running from billyclub charges, I felt that my class at least provided them—however reactionary they were, and some of them were indeed!—with a place to express their shock and con-fusion. The majority were increasingly in sympathy with the aims of the strike (I obliged them to read the Third World manifestos and do some research on the history of the demands and the Administration's response to them), but many had racist attitudes they were scarcely conscious of, and had had no experience of making any personal sacrifice for anything they believed in. Ethically they were savages (as so-called savages are not). The concept of solidarity for an ideal was strange to them. This says a great deal about our non-culture and our educational system. Individually they were nice kids. Within the grave limits of the quarter system (which means that just as one is getting somewhere the course ends) I believe they learned something, morally and socially: at least they were prevented from following their tendency to try to ignore the whole situation as much as they could; they were forced to think about it a bit. A few eventually joined the picket line (I myself picketed every day after the thrice weekly classes, and on most of the Tuesdays and Thursdays in between), and the next quarter I ran into some of them in the People's Park demonstrations. What of the reading and writing skills Freshman English is supposed to be all about? Well, a quarter was not long

enough to ensure radical improvements, in most cases, under
any circumstances; but I don't think their development in this
respect suffered. By the last couple of classes, when, the strike
over (but the class still held in the Newman Center, for by then
I don't think anyone would have preferred to go back to the drab
classroom and its desks), they did in-class writing about a show
of photographs on view in the Gallery room where we met, I felt
that the informality, the tensions we had lived through, and my
encouragement of personal, original, observation and expression of
feeling in their papers, had begun to pay off and that they had a
better idea of what constituted good writing than when we started.

2. Meanwhile I had also been teaching a poetry workshop class
(fourteen students), which I shall not describe in detail since it
did not differ greatly from earlier ones I have already written
about, and to which (since it was held off campus anyway, and
its members were all far more aware and liberated people than
the English 1A students) the strike did not pose any problems.
What did distinguish it (along with the high quality of those
fourteen, as people and as talented poets) was that it met in
rotation in each student's apartment; and this fact added to the
already discussed advantages of meeting in any thoroughly human-
ized setting that of an increased sense, for all of us, of each one's
personal life, of who each one was as expressed by the way he
lived, the pictures he chose to hang or tack on his walls, the books
in his shelves. This increased intimacy deepened our relationships
and gave the class a cohesive quality even greater than that of the
City College class I have described. In the second quarter most
of the fourteen reregistered, and the places vacated by those who
were unable to do so were filled by new students without that
cohesiveness being broken.

In place of the Freshman English, my second course in the second
quarter was an elective seminar, in which we read poetry and
prose by Rilke, Supervielle, Guillevic, William Carlos Williams,
Wallace Stevens, Margaret Avison—with more time spent on Rilke

than on any other. There were thirty students (ten more than I
was obliged to take), chosen by pulling names out of a hat, since
there were seventy-nine or eighty applicants and it was impossible
to interview them all. They were mostly third- and fourth-year
students and—despite the random choice—an astonishingly sensitive, intelligent, responsive bunch; though the group was, alas, too
large and the quarter too short to allow for each one to contribute
and receive to anywhere near the maximum degree. We met—
having been given a ridiculous classroom, the kind in which the
desk-chairs are clamped to the floor—in the cavernous, red-check-
tableclothed coffeehouse of the off-campus Lutheran Center (for
whose hospitality, as for that of the Newman Center, I am
most grateful).

And now I come to the experience from which I learned most
at Berkeley, for which much of what I have just been telling is only
the background, though necessary, I feel, to understanding its
impact:

The People's Park* had, during the first part of the second
quarter, been coming steadily into more and more manifest existence—created by students and "street people"—two blocks away
from our coffeehouse classroom. Many of us had spent some
pleasant time there; a few were actively involved in its construction. I suggested that those from the class who wished to (plus
some from the poetry workshop) meet in the Park one afternoon to
work at digging or planting or whatever was going on. In fact, we
ended up taking a truckload of garbage out to the city dump. In
my poem "From a Notebook" I have written about this:

May 14 1969—Berkeley
Went with some of my students to work in the People's Park.
There seemed to be plenty of digging and gardening help so we
decided, as Jeff had his truck available, to shovel up the garbage
that had been thrown into the west part of the lot and take it
out to the city dump.
       O happiness
       in the sun! Is it

* For documentation of the People's Park events, see *New York Review of
Books* for June 17, 1969.

that simple, then,
to live?
—crazy rhythm of
scooping up barehanded
(all the shovels already in use)
careless of filth and broken glass
—scooping up garbage together
poets and dreamers studying
joy together, clearing
refuse off the neglected, newly recognized,
humbly waiting ground, place, locus, of what could be our New
World even now, our revolution, one and one and one and one
together, black children swinging, green guitars, that energy, that
music, no one
               telling anyone what to do,
               everyone doing,
        each leaf of
        the new grass near us
        a new testament . . .

Out to the dump:
acres of garbage glitter and stink in wild sunlight, gulls
float and scream in the brilliant sky,
polluted waters bob and dazzle, we laugh, our arms ache,
                                we work together
shoving and kicking and scraping to empty our truckload
                                over the bank
even though we know
the irony of adding to the Bay fill, the System has us there—
but we love each other and return to the Park.

This occurred on what turned out to be the last day before the
Battle of Berkeley:

Thursday, May 15th
At 6 A.M. the ominous zooming, war-sound, of helicopters
breaks into our sleep.
To the Park:
ringed with police.
Bulldozers have moved in.
Barely awake, the people—
those who had made for each other
a green place—
begin to gather at the corners.

Their tears fall on sidewalk cement.
The fence goes up, twice a man's height.
Everyone knows (yet no one yet
believes it) what all shall know
this day, and the days that follow:
now, the clubs, the gas,
bayonets, bullets. The War
comes home to us . . .

For almost three weeks thereafter there were daily rallies and
protest marches, with attempts (some at least temporarily successful) to start new Parks on other empty lots; there were many tear-
gassings, police billyclub charges, the naked bayonets of the
National Guard. And always the threat of a repetition of the first
day's buckshot fire when the police killed one young man, blinded
another (an artist), and wounded three hundred more . . . Under
these circumstances, what happened to my classes?

Miraculously, beautifully, even though we found it impossible to
continue our planned reading and discussion of the books on my
list and of students' resulting papers (which sometimes were
poems), yet the larger class (as well as the poetry workshop) continued to meet every Monday, Wednesday, and Friday at 11 A.M.,
usually with full attendance, and often with the addition of some
members of the workshop also. We rapped about the preceding
day's events and life in general—sometimes with reference made
to what we had been reading before the crisis began, or to some
poem or other book that suddenly occurred as relevant—and then
at twelve, instead of continuing till twelve thirty or 1 P.M., we
walked together over to Sproul Plaza for the noon rally and the
afternoon's demonstration. No one put any pressure on anyone else
to come along; but just about everyone did come. And out of these,
a smaller group soon formed that stayed together each day throughout the terror, and most truly—and with a love and mutual care
that made that terror into a time of joy and wonder—practiced the
injunction with which a list of points of conduct and tactics for
the demonstrators, published in the "Instant News" (a sheet dis-
tributed daily at this period from the Free Church), concluded:
"Be your brothers' and sisters' keeper."

What is it that made this experience so important to me even aside from its immediate qualities of drama and emotion? What made it a learning experience for me *as a teacher?* Something like this: Even though, in the brief portion of the quarter that was left after the crisis had abated, the soldiers and sheriffs gone from the streets, and (though the issue had not, and still has not at the time of writing, been settled) things had returned to "normal"— even though, since everyone was deeply shaken, we found it hard to go into our studies again with a certain calm and orderliness that had seemed present when we began, yet I am convinced that if only we had had more time—even if only another month—that class, *which had lived through something important together outside of class meetings*—could have gone further than any I have witnessed. It was only a gleam—a glimpse—but things were said in those last meetings, perceptions were exchanged, not only verbally, but by tone and look and gesture, that attained, or at the least gave promise of, levels of shared learning far beyond the average.

I am not suggesting that we can only teach and learn on the barricades. Indeed, there was very real disruption and distraction of the attention from material we would have liked to explore; no doubt of that. But if some degree of the commonest social intimacy —the exchange of some biographical information, meeting in settings less formal than the classroom, getting to see one another's bookshelves—if even this can make mutual criticism and appreciation and the exchange of insights at once more candid and more sensitive, then the sharing not only of—as in this case—danger, trauma, and the experience of community under provocation—but of all kinds of other realities would surely make shared learning in any field—of the humanities especially—more profound. To have lived through the Berkeley siege means to me, then, not only a new vision of what life might be like in a world of gentle and life-loving people. It means not only the knowledge that there is no such thing as a generation gap when people are engaged in a common task in which they believe. It means not these things alone, though they are much, very much; but also the conviction that a meaning-

ful education in the future—if there is a future worth the name—
will be broken down into the smallest viable units (classes
averaging between ten and fifteen) and that these units will do
many more things together than study specific subjects: they will
cook together (something that would restore meaning to eating
together), and grow vegetables and flowers together, and mend
each other's clothes—and study not only one subject as a group,
but several related and unrelated ones, while each individual
would also be sharing some study and other activities with other
semi-autonomous groups. In such educational interweavings each
teacher would also be, part of the time, a student along with the
rest; and all teachers would share, at least to the extent consonant
with his or her age and family situation, in the life of the commune
—for such educational units would certainly be communes, to a
far greater degree even than such forerunners as Black Mountain
College seem to have been. A pipe dream? I don't believe it is
merely that, remote and hard to effectuate as such a scheme may
sound at a time when colleges everywhere are *expanding.* I can't
see it as a mere pipe dream because I believe it is a necessity. (If
Paul Goodman's proposal for storefront elementary and high schools
had been taken seriously several years ago, it would have been one
of the greatest advances ever made in the history of education.)

The idea of a new kind of college that began to emerge for me,
and for my husband and for two or three young teachers in the
history and political science departments, and which met with great
enthusiasm and useful additional suggestions from the students
with whom I discussed it, involved a minimum capital outlay. Since
classes would all be small, they could be held in people's apart-
ments, a few storefronts, and—for an occasional lecture or assembly
—church halls. All students would work part time and support
themselves as far as possible, so that problems of parental approval
and disapproval would be minimized. Each would pay according
to his ability. Teachers would pool their resources (i.e., inherited
income if any, royalties, income from advisory or other jobs undertaken, etc.) and receive pay according to their need. Need would
have to be evaluated by the community as a whole. Staple foods,

and certain other necessities, could be bought in common.* A day-care center would be established for the children of the community. And a piece of land outside the city would be used to produce food and flowers and as a place for people to go to camp out and rest and breathe fresh air. Administrative staff would be minimal, and, indeed, secretarial work, running Xerox machines, doing janitorial tasks, and so on would provide work for students within the cooperative framework. Obviously plenty of problems would arise (of which the most serious seems to me to be how to provide for the sciences—those which necessitate all sorts of expensive and large laboratory equipment; and perhaps that is an insoluble problem for any very small college (we were envisaging a maximum of, say, two hundred students). But with that exception, are any of them worse problems than the monster institutions we have now are faced with? And would not the existing small colleges be more lively and satisfying places for all concerned if they became teacher-student communes, no longer afflicted with boards of directors, parental anxieties and ambitions, real-estate management headaches, etc., etc., and people were free to teach and learn in an atmosphere of mutual aid?

"And the degrees?" someone asks. "Accreditation?" All I can answer to that is that the most intelligent students I have known care less and less for the degree (here again I am necessarily speaking only of the humanities, I admit) and many quit school before getting it. The basic—perhaps the only—criterion for admission to such a commune/school would have to be that the applicants were interested in sharing their living and learning and that they did not care about ending up with a stamp of approval. Knowing, as they do, these bright, aware, growing individuals of whom every year there seem to be more (if we live . . .), that education as it now exists is as much a part of the Channeling System as the Draft (and I assume most readers of this book will be familiar with the now no longer circulated paper on that topic put out a very few years ago by the Selective Service Department

* I hear that this is now being done by tenants' block unions in Berkeley.

in Washington)—knowing that, there would quite certainly be a more than adequate potential enrollment for my pipe-dream college.

I flew from Berkeley early in June to give the Commencement Address at Bennington College in Vermont. I concluded my speech by suggesting that Bennington turn itself into just such a commune— that faculty, administration, and students pool this (quite considerable) resources, lower their *material* standard of living, and raise their *spiritual* standard of living by sharing, through an "open admissions" policy, the many indisputably good things a Bennington education has to offer. The speech was loudly applauded—but it was not subsequently published, as previous Commencement addresses had been, in the Alumnae magazine. Despite assurances to the contrary, I am unable to believe that this had nothing to do with the proposals I had made. It seems clear that if teachers and students want (and I know there are many, many, who do) the kind of new college I have sketched, there is little hope of persuading existing institutions to change radically in that direction. People are going to have to get together and do it themselves— without big preliminary (and exhausting) fund-raising campaigns, without expectations of each experiment enduring for years and becoming institutionalized (better they should not!), and without wasting time and energy in setting up a lot of rules and regulations and boards of trustees. Let a thousand "hedge schools" bloom.

9

The Word Between Them

WRIGHT MORRIS

A shy, doe-eyed flower-type girl, with braids hanging to her waist, recently submitted to me a sample of her writing talent. The first sentence read, "All f--king men are alike." She was not without talent. As the piece indicated, she was not without experience. Nor was she put off by my comment that the remark was subject to various interpretations. Why not? she asked. Isn't this *creative* writing? Lack of suitable praise led her to drop the course and take up arms in the Peace Corps, who called me to ask how well she would represent us in Afghanistan. On that possibility she thought my judgment more competent.

Somewhere Stendhal says, "If the word love comes up between them, I am lost." This line will serve the writer of fiction who finds himself teaching writing. If the word "creative" comes up—often—he too is lost. It evokes precisely those gifts that lie outside of craft problems. The gifted writer can learn, and does learn, to write better, although most of what he learns is self-taught. He learns by reading writers he considers his superior, and he learns by reading critically what he has written. Without this faculty of self-criticism he will never prove to be his own master. It is also possible for him to learn from the hints and comments of another writer—not too often, perhaps, but it remains within the possible. Considered as *craft,* writing can be taught and most writers can learn to write better. The word "creative" can be left unmentioned.

In the writing program of which I am a member we have courses in Directed Writing. That sensibly and accurately describes the practice. The student assumes he is boundlessly creative, but this gift need not be mentioned. The course consists of interviews dealing concretely with the student's work. The great and ponderable advantage of this arrangement is that the writer is the student's captive public. It exists nowhere else, and he will never know its like again. An actual writer, a published writer, possibly a writer of some distinction and achievement, is committed to reading and appraising the hopeful amateur's performance. Little wonder that writing programs are proving so popular.

Nothing so remarkable can function without its hazards. Every student comes uniquely gifted to exploit this situation, or profit from it. The work is done privately. The confrontation is personal. If the word "creative" doesn't come up between them, most other words do. All require definition. The individual writer in question is seldom using the clichés the student has mastered. He has his own key words. He has his own meaning for these key words. The student's education begins with his effort to fathom what the writer seems to be saying as he underlines words, circles others, or makes cryptic asides in the margins. One of the great appeals of the writing program is that it involves person-to-person confrontation. It is the absolute obverse of the immense herd of students at a distant remove from the famous Professor. In the writing program there he or she is, flesh, voice, and talent. Between student and writer are a few pages of paper concerned with the phenomenon of communication. Education offers little so educational as this—to both the writer and the student. Understandably and unavoidably it also results in non-communication. The issues are crucial. The student asks, Am I any *good?* The pratfalls and the pitfalls are staggering. Everyone knows, including the writer, that the writing program is a catch-all for oddballs, drop-outs, turn-ons, and tune-inners. Every human frailty, most human flaws, can find their day in court in such a program. It can't be helped. It is up to the writer to sort it out. That no two oddballs will prove to be the same is part of his challenge. And it is also true, if infrequent, that the oddest ball may have the soundest talent. All of this can be filed under the education of the writer. The student's education has not yet begun. He has been asked to submit a *fresh* example of his work and it is not out of the question that he might—but if he has an old example that he likes better, he may retype it. It is educational for *him* to hear what this *new* writer thinks of his old work.

This student may be as old, or older, than the writer, with published novels or stories to his credit, or a freshman whose literary background is the collected works of Bob Dylan and the Beatles. The experienced writer may want help with a novel, the perspective afforded by a trained reader, or he may have entered the writing program to take the degree and look forward to teaching other would-be writers.

In the San Francisco area many of the younger students would like to write as they sing, make love, and make revolution. They believe in what comes naturally. Why does writing come so hard? It is not easy to explain that the mind free of the great infirmities of the world of the square may also be free of digested substance, vicarious or real. In simpler terms, empty of much to write about. This predicament, more than taste or inclination, is at the root of the attractions of sex as a subject. It *is* real, and it might be something the student knows something about.

In my experience the student writer is handicapped in wanting to write before he has learned to read. This is as true of the frosh, awakened to the world of books by a long session with *Catch 22*, as it is of the senior citizen who has long been convinced that the "story" she has to tell would make a wonderful movie. For these would-be writers the first step in trying to write is learning to read. The first aesthetic experience of some practical value will be a vague but growing sense of embarrassment. Respectful humility will divert some "talents" from the creative side of writing to the appreciative. Others will knowledgeably proceed at their own risk. The racks of books, the over-abundance of authors, conceals from many would-be writers even the elementary writing problems: the *craft* of fiction may come as a disturbing shock.

A certain percentage of writing students have never suffered courses in *composition*. They attempt, and sometimes do, write a "story" without ever having written a coherent letter. It is not easy for the teacher, in the general disarray of dialogue, description, and irrelevant matter, to put his finger on the *writing* problem. The student has never actually *composed* his thoughts. He may interpret the idea that he *needs* to as a curtailment of his "freedom." He is right. He will find it even harder to grasp, however, that "freedom" has little to do with the craft of fiction. He is the most wrong where he believed himself to be unquestionably right.

The sub-literate student may be a dazzling example of the *media as message*, having been spared, at all levels, the need to put his message into *words*. Again, basic problems of reading precede the serious problems of writing. The new "media literacy" involves other and less specific talents. Fewer impressions and sensations are now dependent on the *written* word.

Can the young man who appreciates *Bonnie & Clyde* on its multiple and contradictory levels bring the same subtle understanding to *Babbitt*, or *Elmer Gantry?* One is language. The other is media. Already the gifted youngster with imagination may feel the *craft* of writing is a waste of time, a half-way step, no more, to where the multiple media of film takes over. It's the *look* that matters. Who cares—or more important, who *remarks*—the refinements of what is *said?*

In the past the apprentice writer took his cues, his style, and sometimes even his subject from the writer he considered his master. Most writers know about this, and that the way out of this dilemma is through it. He keeps up the act until he sees it for what it is.

The young writer of today may not have read enough, or well enough, to have had such a mentor. At the best, among several paperbacks, he has a *favorite*. Joseph Heller, LeRoi Jones, and Albert Camus make a strange but comprehensive constellation. This student writer worships issues, rather than writers, causes rather than authors. His style is less concerned with nuances than with "freedom" of expression. In the writer of fiction this is sex. He tells us all. It is his feeling there is little more to tell. At this point I might suggest *Women in Love* as a volume of possible interest. It may well be the writer's first awareness of the profound complexity of his chosen subject, and may also, with luck, mark the end or the beginning of him as a writer. I have had both.

There is another subject, however, where the student's authority is harder to question. He is on acid. His overpowering subject is the psychedelic hang-up. He wants to tell it like it is. I am his captive audience. As the evidence appears, and tapers off, it is possible, finally, to talk concretely about acid first—then about communications. He has been there, and knows it. I have not. Between us there is nothing but these pages, preferably typed. In this fashion, on his own ground, we have come face to face with the craft problem. It is possible now to talk about writing free of the sentiments we both have about writing. We have these words, and the presence or the absence of some technique. How he felt, what he meant, what he claims to have seen. Is it *there?* Is there a way of getting more of it down than there is? Once the student is sensitized to words as mere slogans, as placards reduced to the function of signs (the four-letter shockers that attest to his freedom), the writer of some talent will seldom again confuse these signs with the craft of fiction. He begins to write prose. If he is a writer, even in this beginning his own voice will emerge from the words he is using. A remarkable mystery. In this tired old world of clichés, something hopefully new.

In contrast to the student who knows nothing, or at the most that he "wants to write," is the amateur savant of extreme sophistication. He has read what matters. He knows more than what he likes. He may have written in several styles, or genres, and be uncertain where his greatest talent lies. This is his problem: not does he have a talent, but where it lies. This also puts him on a footing with the teacher that makes literary discussions possible. He is a reader, and he likes and needs an exchange of views. He often has material submitted to other writers with their appreciative remarks in the margin. He plans to teach. He takes a writing degree with this in mind. There is never much question that he *can* write, and is, by definition, therefore, a writer. There remains the nagging question as to what sort of writer he really is. No category exists for the young intellectual whose talent is to read, to think, and to write about what he thinks. He is in the writing program for the simple reason there is nothing else of interest for him to do. It is also why he makes up his mind to teach. Where else is credit given, and talent respected, for reading, writing, and mere thinking? The only serious requirement is that he must *pass* as a writer—and that isn't too hard. He has read widely and well enough to write like other writers, and in writing about them he learns the craft of writing. He is a young critic on his way to becoming an authority.

My experience as a teacher has led me to modify my distaste for the "therapeutic" side of the writing program. Although we freely assume that the young are in "search" of something, and that the culture should acknowledge and finance these safaris, we are culturally embarrassed to find that the senior citizen is sometimes more at sea than his children—and with reason. It is *his* world, indeed, that the children are breaking up. The established order— so clear to the young, so frequently conjured up for ridicule and attack—is not at all so well established for the older citizens trapped in its ruins. It is a *dis*established order. It serves neither the old nor the young. The senior citizen old enough to sense this may well feel a profound deprivation. His loneliness is indeed more disturbing than that of the long distance runner. Refugees now flowing from these suburban encampments contribute to the crowds of the new campus city. A few who once read, or have turned to reading, are encouraged to feel they can and should *write*. On the imaginative level this is seldom true, but on the personal level the effort may be crucial. This would-be writer uses writing as a means to hold fast to a dissolving order. The creative writing course may well serve as a lifeline for survival. Simple problems of craft are involved in this crisis, but the matters of importance are sublimated. It is an infinitely subtle human crisis concealed beneath an ele-

mentary craft situation. What is worked out may or may not reveal
itself overtly in the writing. What is actually learned about writing
may be of small importance. This "apprentice" has managed to
surface the problems that otherwise have remained unmentioned,
and offer them to a listener on the level of adult discussion. It is a
therapy that works.

For all those who turn to writing as a "creative outlet," recom-
mended as part of a mental hygiene program, the writer-teacher
may serve as an introduction to reading. That *reading* is a talent
usually comes to the student as a surprise. In his "creative" approach to life he has picked up the fashionable creative addiction—
a notion that emotional and intellectual gratification lies only in
writing, painting, dancing, etc. This student would rather write a
mediocre book than make the effort to possess a great one. The
situation is not open to much fruitful discussion, but I have found
it subject to persuasion. *Good* writing does have its effect on those
with either talent or taste. They begin to learn to read. In reading
good writing they may learn to keep silent—or to write better.

No matter how congenial—especially *where* congenial—the
student-writer relationship bristles with hazards. The issue of authority emerges, and the student's eagerness to *share* it with the
writer. It can be assumed that the student is moderately irresolute
or he would not have entered the writing program in the first place.
He wants help. He may well want more help than he should get.
More craft may be necessary to preserve and strengthen the student's faculty for self-criticism, for independent judgment, than is
brought to bear on his writing.

Writing programs now have, like the doctorate programs, un-
countable numbers of hangers-on with their unfinished work in
progress. They shift from teacher to teacher, from program to program: soon enough expanding programs will compete for the most
promising among them. Those less endowed will shift from writer
to writer, looking for the perfect rapport and appreciation. A small
packet of manuscript, some of it bearing the comments of highly
respected writer-teachers, provides this student with his pass and
his rain check. From the captive writer in residence he elicits new

assessments of his old material. He is now less a "promising" writer than a collector of established writers. "But so and so *liked* that one," he says. It is now the writer who is being judged. Writers being human, even generous at moments, they may well advise a student to "keep at it." These may be famous last words. My feeling is they should be dropped from the script. I have a student, now fifty, who thirty years ago was advised, above all, to "keep at it." That was how we talked thirty years ago. Keep at it or bust. This writer has kept at it in the sense that he has never let the promise die. The manuscript in question is approximately the same. Every two or three years it is taken out, a new title page is added, and the first ten or twelve pages are given a going over. It is not bad writing. Worse books are published all the time. This is well known to the author and part of his inexhaustible hope. Once au courant, then passé, the volume now smacks of *historical* interest, and I no longer question that some young editor will "discover" it. In interviews the author will stress that no writer should ever "give up."

My own apprenticeship as a writer was long, unrewarding, and private. In the language of the time, "It tested my character." To be tested in some such manner was the style of my generation. At the heart of this test was the concept of going it alone. To go it alone, relatively unaided, relying on what were described as personal resources, was precisely what made the experience memorable.

There is no question in my mind that an experienced writer-teacher would have profitably shortened my own apprentice experience. What I learned I learned the hard way. There were innumerable things I did not learn. On the basis of craft of fiction alone, going it alone is an expensive indulgence. One man on his own learns too little and often too late. But in the mysterious realms of the imagination that we distinguish by the word "creative," we are often concerned with motivations that precede and exceed the confines of craft. What may be crucial to the writer of talent are not his successes, but his instructive failures, his difficulties. The experience of a *long* apprenticeship may be more valuable than a short one. The early harvesting of what is fresh in the writer, or the premature exploitation of limited experience, may subtly and profoundly exhaust resources that a slower development might have preserved. Beyond the respectful considerations of craft, without which there is no art whatsoever, we are ultimately concerned, as artists, with a uniquely individual vision. Who is to say what elements of experience are crucial to his uniqueness? The frustrations and torments of going it alone are indelibly part of the craft of fiction. It is more difficult to judge what is lost or gained in the writer who is spared these difficulties. The writer who receives professional aid and advice, and goes on to become a successful, admired and productive writer, is hardly the person to speak with insight about the virtues, or vices, of going it alone. It is still an inviolable property of art that it is what it is, and not something else. From whence comes the uniqueness it is the property of craft to make self-evident? If we think of five writers of American fiction —Melville, James, Twain, Crane, and Dreiser—the uniqueness and limitation of each writer are crucial to his own craft problem. To what extent can one *smooth* the way for the writer? I do not know. The question may be impertinent. To talk of an "easy" or a "hard" way is perhaps to talk nonsense. As we increasingly have *easy* ways to live we shall have increased difficulty in writing about it. How much must the writer suffer himself? This is a fundamental problem where the craft of one artist is brought to bear on the craft of another. However casual, it's an intimate relationship.

In place of the long and possibly fruitless apprenticeship of the student writer who goes it alone, we may now have the even longer apprenticeship of the student writer artificially sustained by writing programs. Left on his own, most writers either make it, or give up. In the expanding writing programs it is possible to avoid both extremes. The project goes on. The would-be writer, with his writing degree, soon finds himself instructing other would-be writers. He has found his role. To actually publish something is nice, but it is not necessary to *being* a writer. Becoming a writer is a private ordeal, and quite something else.

My experience has been that the "promising" student, whether young and inexperienced, with relatively no background, or knowledgeably sophisticated, and seriously committed, or older with considerable experience of both writing and living, will usually find that part of his "talent" is his sense of the privacy of his calling. In this new company of writers he must not merely preserve it, but recognize it as the key to his craft problems. He can be helped, but he must rise and sing by himself.

From where he is holed up in the mountains to get on with his novel, I have this word from a young writer: "You're never going to see *me* in some goddam writing program."

I like that. He has my blessings. But his aggressive assurance leads me to wonder. Is it the writer's aid he fears—or his candid opinion of the student's talent? If he never hears such professional advice he can maintain his own illusions longer. Going it alone does not in itself make a talent, or banish the risks.

The writer-teacher can seldom know what it is he does or says that might prove to be useful to the student. Explicitly sometimes, implicitly often, but over the long haul it is by example, the feeling he communicates and shares with the student that the craft they discuss is in the nature of a calling and though many are called few are chosen. If this experience can be shared the writing program need go no further to find its justification, and in the fullness of time there will be good "writers" bearing this stamp.

10

Some Notes on Teaching:
Probably Spoken

GRACE PALEY

Here are about fifteen things I might say in the course of a term. To freshmen or seniors. To two people or a class of twenty. Every year the order is a little different because the students' work is different, and I am in another part of my life. I do not elaborate on plans or reasons, because I need to stay as ignorant in the art of teaching as I want them to remain in the art of literature. The assignments I give are usually assignments I've given myself, problems that have defeated me, investigations I'm still pursuing.

1. Literature has something to do with language. There's probably a natural grammar at the tip of your tongue. You may not believe it, but if you say what's on your mind in the language that comes to you from your parents and your street and friends you'll probably say something beautiful. Still, if you weren't a tough recalcitrant kid, that language may have been destroyed by the tongues of schoolteachers who were ashamed of interesting homes, inflection, and language and left them all for correct usage.

2. A first assignment: To be repeated whenever necessary, by me or the class. Write a story, a first person narrative in the tongue of someone with whom you're in conflict. Someone who disturbs you,

worries you, someone you don't understand. Use a situation you don't understand.

3. No personal journals, please, for about a year. Why? Boring to me. When you find yourself interesting, you're boring. When I find myself interesting, I'm a conceited bore. When I'm interested in you, I'm interesting.

4. This year, I want to *tell* stories. I ask my father, now that he's old and not so busy, to tell me stories, so I can learn how. I try to remember my grandmother's stories, the faces of her dead children. A first assignment for *this* year: Tell a story in class, something that your grandmother told you about a life that preceded yours. That will remind us of our home language. Also—because of time short-age and advanced age, neither your father or your grandmother will bother to tell unimportant stories.

5. It's possible to write about anything in the world, but the slightest story ought to contain the facts of money and blood in order to be interesting to adults. That is—everybody continues on this earth by courtesy of certain economic arrangements, people are rich or poor, make a living or don't have to, are useful to systems, or superfluous. —And blood—the way people live as families or outside families or in the creation of family, sisters, sons, fathers, the bloody ties. Trivial work ignores these two FACTS and is never comic or tragic.

May you do trivial work?

WELL

6. You don't even *have* to be a writer. Read the poem "With Argus," by Paul Goodman. It'll save you a lot of time. It ends:

> The shipwright looked at me with mild eyes.
> "What's the matter friend? You need a New Ship
> from the ground up, with art, a lot of work,
> and using the experience you have—"
> "I'm tired!" I told him in exasperation,
> "I can't afford it!"
>   "No one asks you, either."
> he patiently replied, "to venture forth.
> Whither? why? maybe just forget it,"
> And he turned on his heel and left me—here.

ıcky for art, life is difficult, hard to understand, useless and mysterious. Lucky for artists, they don't require art to do a good day's work. But critics and teachers do. A book, a story, should be smarter than its author. It is the critic or the teacher in you or me who cleverly outwits the characters with the power of prior knowledge of meetings and ends.

Stay open and ignorant.

(For me, the problem: How to keep a class of smart kids—who are on top of Medieval German and Phenomenology—dumb? Probably too late and impossible.)

Something to read: Cocteau's journals.

8. Sometimes I begin the year by saying: This is a definition of fiction. Stesichorus was blinded for mentioning that Helen had gone off to Troy with Paris. He wrote the following poem and his sight was restored:

> Helen, that story is not true
> You never sailed in the benched ships
> You never went to the city of Troy.

9. Two good books to read:

> *A Life Full of Holes,* Charhadi
> *I Work Like a Gardener,* Joan Miro

10. What is the difference between a short story and a novel? The amount of space and time any decade can allow a subject and a group of characters. All this clear only in retrospect.

Therefore: Be risky.

11. A student says—why do you keep saying A Work of Art? You're right. It's a bad habit. I mean to say a Work of Truth.

12. What does it mean To Tell the Truth?

It means—for me—to remove all lies. A Life Full of Holes was said truthfully at once from the beginning. Therefore, we know it can be done. But I am, like most of you, a middle-class person of articulate origins. Like you I was considered verbal and talented and then improved upon by interested persons. These are some of the lies that have to be removed.

1. The lie of injustice to characters.
2. The lie of writing to an editor's taste, or a teacher's.
3. The lie of writing to your best friend's taste.
4. The lie of the approximate word.
5. The lie of unnecessary adjectives.
6. The lie of the brilliant sentence you love the most.

13. Don't go through life without reading the autobiographies of Maxim Gorki

        Prince Kropotkin

            Malcolm X

14. Two peculiar and successful assignments. Invent a person—that is, name the characteristics of a character and all—and we will write about him. Last year it was a forty-year-old divorced policeman with two children.

An assignment called the List Assignment. Because inside the natural form of day beginning and ending, supper with the family, an evening at the Draft Board, there are the facts of noise, conflict, echo. In other years, the most imaginative, inventive work has happened in these factual accounts.

                    For me too.

15. The stories of Isaac Babel and the conversation with him reported by Konstantin Paustovsky in *Years of Hope*. Also, Paustovsky's *The Story of a Life*, a collection of stories incorrectly called autobiography.

Read the Poem "The Circus Animal's Desertion" by William Butler Yeats.

Students are missing from these notes. They do most of the talking in class. They read their own work aloud in their own voices and discuss and disagree with one another. I do interrupt, interject any one of the preceding remarks or one of a dozen others, simply bossing my way into the discussion from time to time because after all, it's my shop. To enlarge on these, I would need to keep a journal of conversations and events. This would be against my literary principles and pedagogical habits—all of which are subject to change.

Therefore: I can only describe the fifteen points I've made by telling you that they are really notes for beginners, or for people like myself who must begin again and again in order to get anywhere at all.

11

Want to See My Bottom?

L. S. SIMCKES

Two basic contexts, the world inside or close to the student and the world distant and perhaps alien. Two centers of attention, the family and the stranger. I take it as my *initial* task to push each student to see, on the one hand, the particular drama of his own family and, on the other, the possible dramas in the lives, only partially shown to him, of strangers. At the outset, therefore, I give my students the following two assignments. I ask them to write (not mail) a letter of accusation to a member of their family, preferably the mother or father, in which they bring up all the details of resentment, disappointment, blame, they can remember and analyze—Kafka's long, nearly novella-size, unmailed letter to his father, published as "Dearest Father," is a document I encourage them to read in this connection. The simple importance of such a letter is that the student is addressing somebody, for the trouble often with the early stories students write is that they lack the poignancy of an immediate necessity. Why is the story being told, the reader wonders, and to whom? The student may be hampered from creating an imaginative natural voice because an audience is missing. The letter is a bridge to fiction. The complex importance, however, of such a letter is not just that the student is talking about what he knows and feels, but also that in exposing the genealogy, as it were, of his being he is breaking a taboo of shyness. He is telling me, a stranger, secrets. The business of art, though, is giving away secrets.

As a second assignment, I ask them to prepare at least five pages of eavesdropping upon strangers. I expect them to pay murderous attention to the conversation and action of people of varied ages at restaurants, bars, on streets, until something about these strangers is revealed to them, until something hits them. To make out some case concerning these people, whether drunks or children, after the manner say of Dostoyevsky who had a passion for following strangers like a detective and making shrewd guesses about them. Of course, the student may take wrong or weird suggestions from his few observed facts, from his collection of gestures, voices, clothes; a hand always jumping to an eye may hint that the person before him is playing at being sick, or it may evoke, for all I know, the image of a train crossing a bridge. The point is that the revelation is double. Something about the stranger may be revealed, but something also about the student. And the object of a writing class is to enable a student to find out what interests him, what excites his imagination, and what is exciting about his own imagination. Sometimes, too, the imagination, following its own interests, discovers curious truths. During an office hour, a student once told me about her angers against her mother, angers stuck from the days of childhood when her mother would insult her in front of others. I suggested that she write a story in which, perhaps, an intense precocious child, in order to get back at her mother, drops pieces of paper around the house and the yard, for anybody to pick up, notes condemning her mother. The girl stared at me and said, "That's what I did. I dropped them everywhere."

Both assignments meet much resistance. As for the letter, one student at Harvard said it was "metaphysically bad, morally bad, and bad all around," because the parent would have no chance to reply. Do you fantasize? I asked. He did. Do you have fantasies in which you carry on arguments against your parents? He did. Do you give them a chance to reply? He didn't. Subsequently he submitted two brilliant letters, five pages to a parent, ten to a friend, and his later fiction inherited much of the energy and freedom present in his letters. A girl at Vassar insisted that she was interested not in the *givens* of her life but in her own private *choices:* her family was something given to her, her loves were something she herself chose. As for eavesdropping, one Harvard student, as soon as he heard the assignment at our first meeting, got up, shouted "It's a sin!" retrieved his sample manuscripts, and left for good.

So far I have been speaking of *initial* shoves, initiatory pushes into certain directions. The ultimate burden of discovery lies in the domain of the student's luck and ambition. My intention is not to bully or enslave. Right off I announce that I always keep in an important pocket my agreement with Sir Joshua Reynolds that "Few are taught to any purpose who are not their own teachers." I claim, they must teach me as much as I teach them, teach me *before* I teach them. I say, they have the right to insist upon their own ways despite the advice of any teacher just as I have the right to insist on my ways despite them. In any case, I try to throw away the whip of grades. I try not to be the dog obeyed in office. My first two years of teaching, it is true, I gave out a total of two D's. But the third and fourth years, no lower than a C. And the fifth, B was my floor. Next year I expect to give all A's, and as soon as possible thereafter no grades whatsoever. On the one hand, my progress as a teacher has been toward a willingness to impose a personal or eccentric scheme upon my class, and, on the other, to have that scheme upset by anything improvised by the students which is exciting. Each class must help invent the pattern of its own schooling. One day, at Vassar, I ended a class with the joke that we would meet next time under the table. And, the next time we met, there they were, under the big table, where I joined them. To be sure, this was somewhat silly, but the ladder toward creation is long and it takes, sometimes, a few foolish steps. Once, just once, I brought in three toy figures, a Norwegian yokel and a Japanese boy and girl with springy heads. And we sort of played dolls. Objects can be handled; language lacks a certain tangibility. By playing with these toy people, suggestions emerged concretely and immediately. Place the yokel in between the Japanese couple, you have perhaps the man who brought them together or the man who may break them apart. Knock the yokel to the ground, other possibilities sud-

denly exist—betrayal, death, dreaming. *Where* a person is helps to
establish *what* a person is. My aim was to free their attitudes toward their own material. Let them deal with what they are extremely familiar but let them also take advantage of their freedom
to translate, transpose, invent, in accordance with other commitments and compulsions, alien perhaps to preliminary givens. Let
them also write about a country they've never been to, except in
some fantasy.

At Stanford, in its less cosmopolitan or experimental days (1960–
61), I began my teaching. I was a Teaching Fellow for Freshman
English. *Oi vai!* The trouble was, we were encouraged to teach in
some (though not absolute) accordance with a text book. I understood that the more we relied on it, the more were we blessed. But
using it was always a trick and an embarrassment, and after the
rhetoric book came the casebook. From description, boys and girls,
to argument, to research! Instead of twisting my days into such a
shape, I should have rebelled completely. For instance, to me it
makes more sense to start a year of Freshman English by allowing
the students, individually or collectively, to select some writer that
interests them. Thereafter the agreement would be, as they read the
man's works and life, they follow as many other interesting or unfamiliar references or leads as possible. They'd go from link to link,
jump from item to item, the way you would if you were looking up
a word in a dictionary and came across another unfamiliar word—
you'd look up that word too. Learning takes place best when you
need to learn, when something arrives to explain something else,
when one thing actually leans on another. What should always be
avoided is that paper fan, that schematic spread which encourages
a concern for patching up holes in one's knowledge as an act of
protection against insult or social stigma or, worse, college failure.
So, a student beginning with a modern figure would obviously be
led to some art of an earlier period, and not necessarily literary
art. Keats might point to the medieval ballad or Greek art. There
would certainly be an explosion of references, a chaos of sorts, the
center might not hold. But, after all, until there is sufficient chaos
there is no need to talk of order. Chaos is a sign of chaos, but also a
sign of coming order. Introducing order too soon is as bad as in-

troducing it too late. Perhaps the greatest benefit of this kind of approach is not just that each student has his own course but that the teacher himself is taking his own course. In this context, information becomes excitement, becomes insight, and the dictum of Sir Joshua is heeded all around.

When I was a student, my teacher told me: "Give the reader time to know your characters. Introduce them one at a time. Slow down." As if he were some speech therapist and I the poor fellow whom others would understand if only I learned to speak more slowly. The advice is kind and good, but like any rule in art, when followed too closely, it threatens to pinch the neck of discovery. A story can get the reader to read it in almost any way it wants; at least it can try. If a student's most interesting work emerges from a deep sense of fantasy where motivation is ruthlessly or comically inadequate, there is no place any more for the conventional though useful demand for motivation. Order enters the writing class as it enters a story, experimentally, tentatively. It is ultimately the last thing created although being created all the time.

For myself, I want something more intense, more chaotic, than the usual informality and relaxation of a writing class. I want the crater of art to be hot. Rules tend to go cold, but perhaps not personal ones. At Vassar, after my having stressed the priority of "bad" experiences, i.e., confusion, pain, failure, embarrassment, these must be exposed and handled first, i.e., without an acknowledgement of despair and fantasy the language of hope and reality is dishonest, a student complained that if she tried to write a "sad" story it would come out all wrong, she had nothing tragic to tell, she was a very happy person. The story she had already handed in was the tale of her witty, energetic grandmother. It turned out, however, that her grandmother was in fact not merely senile but grotesquely immobile. And as for herself, before school started she had jumped out of a moving car, luckily only breaking a leg. I should add that her speaking voice had one peculiarity, it always sounded as though she was crying. For a vision to have depth and truth, it must deal with pain. But pain, it must be remembered, is the source of comedy as well as tragedy, *contra* Aristotle. That laughter and grief are both necessary is an important discovery. Cruelty is not the only outcome of an honest encounter with one's own experience. A writer's vision is as brutal as it is tender. This girl ultimately wrote a poignant monologue of comic self-abasement, called "The Hawker," in which the speaker pleads to give everything she has away: "Hey, anybody need a favor? Just ask. . . . Want to use a phone? Use mine. I'll leave the room . . . Here, take my chair. Go on. I'll be sitting on the floor anyway so you might as well prop your feet upon my shoulders." Her last piece of prose was a letter to me in which she declares herself mad. Also in the letter was the title for a story which she unfortunately never managed to write: "What would it look like if I were a stranger?" In short, a student of mine is encouraged to imagine the extreme; I agree with Dürrenmatt, a story is not complete until it has taken its worst possible turn.

A further priority—the priority of oral language, the spoken word. Children are able to use their imaginations when speaking but less so when writing. Because the rhythms of the imagination are too often subject to punishment under the school rules of decorum and diction. A second-grader talking about the kick of a gun said to me: "It pulls back, like when you're walking and the guy pulls you back." This precise little image is liable to be erased in a classroom. Standards of expected or correct usage simply rob children of their own ways of saying things, and their own ways are usually inventive, ambitious, exciting. No wonder many students enter college empty-handed. Rhetoric, it should be pointed out everywhere, has colloquial as well as academic sources. We say, "Tomorrow I'll see you, I'll see you tomorrow," and that's an example of, heaven help us, *epanalepsis*. I asked a four-year-old girl how big her brother was; she answered: "He's up that high." I asked her why she had a bandaid on her finger; she answered: "My meat is opened." One child at a nursery for "disadvantaged" children came up to me all of a sudden and screamed: "What's a buddy stuck in your ear?" "What do you mean?" I said. He said: "It means you're upside down and a little beer in your mouth and you're crying so hard." Fantasy, babbling, disturbed nonsense, are important places of energy for language to appear—and in an uninhibited though maybe difficult fashion. But art is difficult communication. One day I had my Vassar class talk, or rather babble, facing the wall, one by one. That is, I wanted to break down for the moment their reliance upon a realistic situation as the occasion for language, I wanted to astonish them with their own complicated resources, with the possibility in their own mouths for rich strange language. It was difficult, and I didn't pursue it enough. Some students, misunderstanding me, sounded like Shakespeare's Pyramus with his "O wall!" My mistake was, I didn't try it again.

Why not try the following? (I intend to.) Ask a student to make up a story in class and then have the others heckle, or argue against him. If he says, So-and-so was a short old man, you yourself shout out, That's a lie, he was tall and young. The hard job of convincing an audience, of adding details, metaphors, images, will slap the storyteller in the face. Let everybody argue back and forth, boast back and forth, tall-tale fashion, kid-stuff fashion. For what purpose? Under these circumstances, (playfully) insulting circumstances, the storyteller may be forced in class to invent more convincingly. In any case, the problem of convincing an audience, of finding the appropriate and necessary details for a story, is dramatically there.

What releases another's language and imagination is something of a mystery—in my case, one certain key is the approach to madness, so it is natural for me to throw my students somewhat in that direction. In my fiction, God is a bum. Once I asked my students to shut their eyes and then write down whatever they saw. In this private world behind our own eyes, the pace of metamorphosis is amazing. But sometimes you can wait an hour before the visions come, like waiting strike time for a Long Island train. It might have been better had each student told his visions to another student who would act, for the time being, as amanuensis to the prophet. Anyway, despite the near illegibility of their blind script, it was a good idea to let their minds wander, let them daydream in class to their own benefits. A very familiar thing became strange to them. I was interested in showing them they could write about anything. Again, to show my students that the narrative imagination takes hints from all places, to encourage them to include anything in their stories, I read a small passage from Wittgenstein's *Blue Book:*

> Suppose I pointed to a piece of paper and said to someone:
> "this colour I call 'red.' " Afterwards I give him the order: "now
> paint me a red patch." I then ask him: "why, in carrying out my
> order, did you paint just this colour?"

Then I myself ask: Is there anything dramatic here, anything that
suggests some particular relationship? After a while, somebody
catches what I am after, the tyranny in the voice of the speaker. To
tell a person to do something and then ask him why he has done
it, that is a form of interrogation which might issue from the realm
of espionage. Or it might signal a babyish or senile approach to
another human being, or the magician's way with his prepared
hoaxes. Wittgenstein's "philosophical investigation" of the justifications we have for any act amounts to a kind of torture. A classroom itself, with its constant questions, could inspire terror, with
its dialectics, one will breaking another, one will embarrassing
another. Isn't Wittgenstein's passage a parody of a reign of terror?
Given such authority and such vulnerability, anybody can turn you
around, make it impossible for you to act or think about your
actions, drive you crazy.

You may feel that the only decent and direct way to get students
to write is to let them alone altogether until they come up with
something, until they find their stories and the language adequate
for these stories. Why antics and pranks? In part I agree with you.
But I am talking about beginners, who need shaking. At Vassar,
after the letter assignment, the best work adopted the form of a
message or a plea, to somebody expected or gone or dead. The
assignment worked. I have had students whose early work was
silly and whose final work was so good the class confused it with
the work of the class master. Certainly what shook these "late
bloomers" most was being exposed to the style and performance
and conversation of other students, but also what helped was
stepping on the crazy ground of the course itself. With one hand
I push my students away, so they'll be on their own, with the other
I force them to need me.

In his 1887 *Myth, Ritual, and Religion* Andrew Lang tells of an
American who, living among Amazons in order to take down their
myths, was unable to get the Indians to tell him a single story, not

by coaxing, not by offers of money. Once, however, he overheard a steersman telling his oarsmen a story to keep them awake. Thereafter, when the American told this story to other Indians, they responded by relating a story to him. The simplest way, perhaps, to get students to tell you stories is by first telling them your own. In this respect I have been a tiny bit delinquent. I've assigned my fiction or encouraged students to read it, but not yet read it in class.

All the teacher is trying to do is make the student accessible to himself, make him as bold as possible. That, though, is an enterprise bound, in many cases, to encourage resistance. A resistance of a strange sort. Once I asked a class to compose a list of their own shames, not to be handed in, and a student wouldn't begin until I assured him again that the material was not required to be submitted. But when he was through, this student handed in his list. In truth, the more I have helped my students be accessible to themselves and the more I have used my imagination to release theirs, I have found myself fearing that I myself may become less accessible to myself, have less imagination for my own purposes. And with fear comes anger. Such nightmares, however, are inevitable, like fearing you'll turn academic if you teach one course. Certainly this fantasy of robbing myself to pay my students is not the whole story. The rabbis say that when God smashed the first Temple he said he had bad students, and when he smashed the second he admitted he was a bad teacher. I haven't smashed any temples yet.

To conclude, an important agreement between student and teacher is that the student not be shy and the teacher not be angry. Most of the time anyway. A few years ago, while I was visiting a certain rabbi, his five-year-old daughter suddenly asked me, "Want to see my bottom?" Her father and mother present, I said: "Yes, certainly!" So she turned round, lifted her dress, and—since she was wearing no underwear—there at once was her bottom. "Oh," I said, "what a lovely bottom!" So she let the hem of her dress go, turned back round to face me, and raising now the front hem to her mouth said: "I'm sort of shy." Of course, there at once was her shy, or actually sly, side. The lesson? A shy side may be bolder than a bold side.

JONATHAN BAUMBACH, who has a Ph.D. in English and American Literature from Stanford University, has taught writing at Stanford, Ohio State University, New York University, and Brooklyn College, and presently is a visiting writer-in-residence at Tufts University. He has published two novels, *A Man to Conjure With* and *What Comes Next;* a textbook, *Moderns and Contemporaries* and a critical study, *The Landscape of Nightmare.* His soon-to-be-completed new novel is called *Dream Book.*

WENDELL BERRY is a Kentuckian, teaching at the University of Kentucky, living in the town of Port Royal. He has published two novels, *Nathan Coulter* and *A Place on Earth;* a book of essays, *The Long-Legged House;* and three books of poems, *The Broken* has published two novels, *A Man to Conjour With* and *What Comes Ground, Findings,* and *Openings.* A new book of poems, *Farming: A Hand Book,* will shortly be published.

ROBERT CREELEY has taught at Black Mountain College, University of New Mexico, University of British Columbia, and is presently Professor of English at the State University of New York at Buffalo. Mr. Creeley was the editor of the *Black Mountain Review* during the time of its publication (1954–57) and is the author of *For Love* (Poems, 1962); *The Island* (A novel, 1963); *The Gold Diggers* (Stories, 1965); *Words* (Poems, 1967); *Pieces* (Poems, 1969); *A Quick Graph* (Critical notes and essays, 1969); and *The Charm* (Early poems, 1969).

GEORGE P. ELLIOTT has taught English, including creative writing, at St. Mary's College (California), Cornell University, Barnard College, University of Iowa (Writer Workshop), University of California (Berkeley), and, since 1963, Syracuse University, as well as at a number of summer writers conferences. He has published, in addition to book reviews and articles in a variety of journals, three novels, *Parktilden Village, David Knudsen,* and *In the World;* two collections of short stories, *Among the Dangs* and *An Hour of Last Things;* one collection of poems, *From the Berkeley Hills;* and one collection of essays, *A Piece of Lettuce.*

GEORGE GARRETT was born in 1929 in Orlando, Florida, and was educated at Princeton University. Since the publication of *The Reverend Ghost: Poems* in 1957, he has published three novels, three collections of short stories, two other collections of poems, and a play; he also edited the anthology *The Girl in the Black Raincoat.* Currently Professor of English at Hollins College, Mr. Garrett has taught at Wesleyan, Princeton, Rice, and the University of Virginia. He was recipient of the Sewanee Review Fellowship in Poetry, The Rome Prize of American Academy of Arts and Letters, and in 1960 a Ford Foundation Grant in Drama.

IVAN GOLD was born in New York City in 1932. He graduated from Columbia College, served in the U.S. Army in Japan, and received a degree from the School of Oriental and African Studies, University of London. A collection of short stories, *Nickel Miseries,* was published in 1963. His novel, *Sick Friends,* from which the present piece on teaching was excerpted, was published in 1969. Mr. Gold has taught fiction writing at Columbia University.

JOHN HAWKES was born in Stamford, Connecticut, in 1925. He taught writing for three years at Harvard and, since 1958, has been at Brown University where he is presently a Professor of English. In 1966 he served on The Panel on Educational Innovation in Washington, D.C., and that same year directed an experiment in Freshman English ("Voice Project") at Stanford. He is a Guggenheim fellow and has received grants from the Ford Foundation, the Rockefeller Foundation, and the National Institute of Arts and Letters. His novels include *The Cannibal, The Lime Twig,* and *Second Skin.* He has published a volume of short plays, *The Innocent Party,* and recently his stories and short novels appeared in a collection entitled *Lunar Landscapes.*

DENISE LEVERTOV, much-celebrated poet whose latest volume of verse is *Relearning the Alphabet,* is now teaching at MIT, about which she says, "the furthest possible thing from a hedge school, but I have—again!—exceptionally fine students, and I feel it is as important to work from within the existing institutions as to create models of a new education outside them; indeed, to create such models, as far as one is able, in individual classes, may, one hopes, stimulate some students eventually to go out and develop their own new schools. There are many teachers here whom I admire and respect, and who are fighting the warmachine aspects of this place—"

WRIGHT MORRIS is the author of fourteen novels, including the 1957 National Book Award winner *The Field of Vision, Ceremony in Lone Tree, One Day, In Orbit;* three photo-text books, the most recent of which is *God's Country and My People;* a book of criticism, *The Territory Ahead;* and a collection of his writings, *Wright Morris: A Reader.* Mr. Morris is a Guggenheim fellow and the recipient of grants from the National Institute of Arts and Letters and the Rockefeller Foundation. He is currently on the faculty of San Francisco State College where he lectures on the novel and teaches in the creative writing department.

GRACE PALEY is not an academic person—that is, she never finished college, though the last six years has lived an academic life. She has taught at Sarah Lawrence, Columbia, and Syracuse. Her book, *The Little Disturbances of Man,* was reissued in 1968 by Viking and Bantam. Her stories have appeared in such places as *Esquire, Atlantic Monthly, Genesis West, Win, Icon*—She has been the recipient of a Guggenheim award and a National Foundation of Arts and Humanities Grant.

L. S. SIMCKES has taught at Stanford, Vassar, Harvard, and is now an Assistant Professor at the Harvard Graduate School of Education where he teaches a course in experimental narrative-and-play writing. His novel, *Seven Days of Mourning,* has been adapted as a play and other work includes short stories, critical essays, and translations from the Hebrew.